What Love Is *Not*

A Premarital Handbook for Couples
How Not to Fail in a Marriage
A Perspective from Two People Who've Failed . . . and Tried Again

CASSIDY AND DANIELA PARLANE

ISBN 978-1-64140-550-8 (paperback)
ISBN 978-1-64140-551-5 (digital)

Christian Faith Publishing, Inc.
832 Park Avenue
Meadville, PA 16335
www.christianfaithpublishing.com

Printed in the United States of America

Contents

Introduction

From the perspective of two people who have lived through divorce, we will not pretend to have all the answers to the marriage relationship. What we can tell you is how *not* to fail in a marriage. In life, the best person who qualifies to tell someone else how not to fail at something would be one who himself failed at one point or another at that thing. For instance, the first lightbulb was invented by Humphry Davy in the early 1800s. Many of us may not have heard of him because what's more important is not so much his name as it is the thing he invented. A more familiar name would be Thomas Edison, an American inventor, scientist, and businessman who then purchased the patent and later improved the invention. The story went on to say "It took him 1,000 times to make the lightbulb. He said he didn't fail 1,000 times; he found 999 ways not to make a lightbulb." Charles Kettering went on to say, "An inventor fails 999 times, and if he succeeds once, he's in. He treats his failures simply as practice shots."

You don't need to fail 999 times to get it right, but if you have failed in the past, hopefully, you will have learned a few things going forward. There is often a stigma or sense of unworthiness that comes with being divorced—thankfully, there is hope because of God's amazing grace. This is what has propelled us to write this book in order to demonstrate God's complete restoration power. While there are those who may have not experienced the great tragedy that comes with divorce, they may have experienced low points or even a constant survival-mode state of mediocrity. The spark has been snuffed out. Marriage has been merely reduced to a monotonous routine. For some, marriage may have flatlined. This book seeks to revitalize, restrengthen, and bring hope to the institution of marriage that

God so loves. This book is filled with nuggets of truth that we have learned along our journeys to encourage you—wherever you are in the process of marriage. Whether you are single and thinking about marriage, engaged, or married, these principles are applicable to all.

Our prayer is that you will begin to live a more fulfilled and enriched life in your relationship with God, first and foremost, and with your spouse.

Prayer of Hope

Dear Lord Jesus,

We ask that you will be the center of our lives as we seek to obey you in all that we do. We acknowledge that we cannot do anything in our own strength that will experience true success outside of you. This includes our marriage, our family, our home, our career, our dreams, and all that we desire. We surrender and lay it all down at the cross. We ask for your perfect will to be done. Restore what needs to be restored. Bring life to what once lived. Give us fervor, give us passion, and give us the will to love our spouse us you love us. Amen.

Chapter 1

What Love Is Not

We often do all the things *love* is not and expect the results of what *love* is. Just as how our bodies need water and other essential nourishments for a healthy life, every relationship requires the vital components of love. It is love that fuels the marriage relationship long after the wedding day and the honeymoon are over. Is love a natural feeling or a common reaction we exhibit toward one another as humans? Trying to define *love* is not as simple as one may first perceive. Love, in all its glory and attributes, is a divinely complex force. We assimilate behavioral patterns that exist in our present spheres of influence from childhood. These patterns help shape many misconceptions about love and what it is or isn't. As a result, these behaviors, if not dealt with from earlier on in life, may translate and manifest in each relationship that we form throughout our lifetime. Love's possibilities are endless. The potential for all to discover true love is vast yet attainable. In light of its discovery, it is the human spirit that holds the key to love and all its essences. No matter how hard we try to hide behind a mask, love will always unveil our true person. It's like sweeping dirt under a rug: the dirt is still there, and it will remain there long after, if no one uncovers it and makes a conscious effort in cleaning it up. When the human spirit meets love, the force that is created will always surface the hidden person, good or bad.

Love Is *Not* Impatient

Every waking moment of life, love is put to the test. One of the fundamental principles that love depends on for growth is the virtue of patience. How do we expect patience to do its perfect work in and through us if all we do is run ahead of its process? Our impatience often speaks to the level of maturity we possess or the lack thereof. Much like raising a child or kick-starting a business, it takes an enduring patience to see the end results of one's labor. The same is true for a relationship. Every relationship, particularly a marriage, requires patience for growth. Marriage is the classroom that gives its participants the opportunity each day to learn what it means to be patient.

Observe a child: even before he is able to speak, he cries in hopes to communicate discomfort, frustration, or his desire to be held. He wants it now, no questions asked. The same is true in a marriage where things aren't happening fast enough, whether it is in the area of finances, career goals, or what have you. The difference here is that we have the ability to choose how we react. In a world of instant gratification, impatience is "the norm." It's a world that offers a multiplicity of options. On the contrary, these options, as it were, pose a threat to healthy and balanced relationships, which require a great deal of perseverance for achieving even the smallest degree of success.

Can you recall moments in prayer while exclaiming the simple words "Lord, I need more patience"? Why is it that once those words are uttered, they never go unanswered? All hell breaks loose, and you end up in circumstances that drive you to develop patience. God indeed works in mysterious ways and surely has a sense of humor. Is life constantly teaching us lessons that we fail to observe or learn? Are we too caught up in getting what we want and nothing else? Do we have the innate power to control not just our impatience but our response to the tests thereof? More often than we would admit, we buckle under pressure as humans and somehow find a way of escape. Subsequently, we will undoubtedly find ourselves repeating the test of patience until we pass it. There is no way of skipping the test. Overcoming impatience requires a disciplined mind-set. Impatience is the absence of temperance. Persons with this behavior tend to occasionally display aggression toward their spouse and may find themselves in situations they never expected. These are circumstances that will eventually magnify themselves over time. We must develop a mind-set that cultivates a balanced perspective on life that causes us to think and act rationally.

Love Is Not Unkind

There are principles in life that are unchangeable. One of those principles is the age-old golden rule. It cannot and, most importantly, will not change in order to custom-fit our theology or way of life. We must treat those we love and people as a whole with the same dignity and humanity as we would like to be treated. The marriage relationship and all other affiliations in our lives thrive and flow from this principle. When the golden rule is lived out, it becomes much easier for it to be reciprocated. We receive what we put out. In other words, our intake is a result of our output. Let us not be deceived in our thinking. Whatever we sow, we will reap. In a marriage, it is very easy for parties to become unkind or nasty toward one another. Certainly, this type of behavior is never acceptable on any level. Sarcasm, cynicism, and condescension fuel a negative attitude, resulting in unkindness. This blocks the flow of healthy communication. It is even harder for intimacy to be sustained when this behavior is perpetuated. How does one overcome the temptation of being unkind? Does this describe the person you really are? Is marriage the cause of who you've become? Have you become unrecognizable to your spouse as a result? If you look in the mirror and the person you see is highly unrecognizable, then you may need to do an introspective look. We all have blind spots in our lives, and sometimes, it takes another person to reveal hidden behavioral patterns we have overlooked.

Love Does *Not* Envy and It Does *Not* Boast

"And they two shall be one flesh" (Mark 10:8) clearly states a position of unity. How can some people envy their own selves? When envy is propagated in a relationship, if it is not stopped in its tracks, it will cause vicious cycle. The success of one party in the marriage relationship reflects the success of the other. No one is superior. Now that you are married, all single mentality is abandoned. You are a complement to your partner, not a competition. How then can you envy the one you love, the one with whom you are one? Envy happens more frequently than we can imagine. Envy is a silent killer;

for instance, the wife earns a higher salary than her husband does. The man then feels obligated to be the higher earner, which could lead to deep envy toward his own wife. This type of built-up envy may never be admitted by the husband, of course. A man's envy is not easily provoked, but a little envy is envy nonetheless. The marriage relationship always starts off with good intentions, where both parties dream of great successes together while wishing nothing but the best for each other. But somewhere along their journey together, they sometimes discover that good intentions aren't always enough to save the day. Couples should get to the place where they celebrate each other and not just tolerate each other. It is okay if one earns more than the other, be it the wife or the husband. This also happens if one is more gifted than the other. Find the joy in building up each other. Learning to accept each other's strengths and weaknesses has its advantages. It's difficult for a marriage to function as it was intended when there is envy at its core.

There is not a bone of jealousy where love is concerned. Jealousy or envy breeds boastfulness. Why boast? All that you possess belongs not only to you but also to your partner, with whom you have committed living the rest of your life. You share in both your successes as well as your failures. When parties become boastful, it results in an undertone of arrogance. No one likes being around an arrogant person. True or false? Can you see where the door for ongoing conflict is left open here? No one knows you better than your spouse. They are the first to detect the slightest appearance of boastfulness or arrogance. This creates tremendous friction; it even crushes all possible options for parties to work effectively together on any team initiatives. At this place, nothing that is done would ever be good enough for the other. Whenever the team environment is threatened, the entire marriage is riding on a very slippery slope. It is said that "behind every good man, there is a good woman" or "behind every good woman, there is a good man." Strive to foster a healthy home base where there is support and encouragement. There must never be a situation where compliments and support are only found outside the home. Why should your partner say things such as "My friends show me more support than you have ever shown throughout this whole marriage" or "Why do you think I stop what I am doing and leave as soon as you enter the room?" or "I'm happier at work than I am at home"? It is never easy to hear those words, but we must endeavor to protect the unity of our marriage. By eliminating envy and the need to boast, your marriage will be on the path to greatness. Pulling each other down solves nothing.

Love Is *Not* Proud

There is nothing prideful about love. Pride can be expressed in two different contexts: a negative one and a positive one. Let's focus on the negative context. Pride can mean someone has an exaggerated sense of self-accomplishment, resulting in arrogance and disrespect toward others. According to Proverbs 16:18, "pride goes before destruction," which means that if someone is too conceited or egotistic, something will happen to make you look foolish. Strong words, but true. So then, if we say we love, why do we allow pride to get the best of us, which, in turn, creates a great divide in relationships? Pride is subtle. Our society has taken what remains the great sin of humanity and has given it a rather watered-down definition. In today's self-indulgent society, when someone says "I feel proud of myself," it is seen as a culturally accepted expression. From childhood, it is instilled in us to be proud of ourselves, to follow *our* dreams and put our wants on a pedestal. There is nothing innately good about pride, so for our culture to use the term *proud* with the things relating to love, it is clear why the expression is so ingrained; hence, it's common use in our everyday language. Love and pride are polar opposites. Yet pride finds a way in our lives. Here are examples of potential open doors:

1. Unresolved situations in the marriage resulting in unforgiveness: "I don't need to make the first move because it wasn't my fault."
2. Someone in the marriage not yet learning that there is no "I" in team: "I will chase my dreams with or without you."

3. Arrogance or egos left unchecked: "I'm not the one who needs counseling."

4. Esteeming oneself higher than one ought to (Romans 12:3): "I'm independent! I can do it on my own."

5. Education or career status : "If it wasn't for me, you'd be nothing!"

6. One's circle of association: "What would our friends think if they saw us living in *that* house?"

7. Self-pity: "I wish I had *her* body. I hate how fat I look."

Pride is an area in life that we all have to contend with. Once it is dealt with on a personal level, it fosters growth. A person who has made relentless efforts in dealing with pride issues, be it personally or in a marriage situation, has done a world of justice for any relationship he may find himself in. That which he fails to openly or privately deal with will undoubtedly move stealthily up on him when he least expects it. Whenever an individual is proud, he cannot see his own faults. Pride is deceptive and will always cover one's blind spot. Why is it that we are often quick to see the pride in others and not in ourselves? Evidently, it becomes devastating in a marriage when the person in the wrong cannot admit to it. Sometimes the only antidote to this behavior is time itself. The proud will always find a reason to put the blame on others. The aftermath of pride can be unrecoverable. When pride is detected in the marriage, each party must make a conscious effort to crush its cancerous root. Do not wait too long before dealing with pride. Pride will always seek to pull down or cause shame. Put your pride to shame. Do not wait for your pride to put you to shame.

Love Does *Not* Dishonor

Dishonor can destroy the home front as fast as a widespread tsunami could destroy an island. Love does not dishonor. The word *dishonor* is used synonymously with the word *disrespect*. Dishonor creates weak links. All on its own, it dismisses boundaries and disintegrates foundations. It alienates and creates victims. Its kryptonite could suck the life out of the marriage relationship in the most excruciating ways. For the most part, it is often not intentional in its approach, yet it could slowly and painfully kill every cell there is in any relationship. A couple that builds their marriage on the principles or practices that involves dishonor is sure to experience the absence of peace throughout the life of that marriage. Respect is one of the pillars of marriage, resulting in longevity. Dishonor does the very apposite. Couples need to understand that by dishonoring their spouse, they are dishonoring their own selves. Here are some examples of dishonor/disrespect in the marriage:

1. Swearing at each other
2. Hiding secrets/betrayal
3. Lying
4. Manipulation
5. Name-calling
6. Comparing your spouse to others in a negative way
7. Sarcasm/cynicism/narcissism (a negative attitude)
8. Sharpness of the tongue (rude responses), etc.

In a place of dishonor, couples may find themselves exhibiting these examples given throughout their marriage more often than they would admit. It is always in the best interest of the marriage that couples should seek the appropriate counseling to at least begin the process in finding healthy resolutions.

Love Is *Not* Self-Seeking

Me, myself, and I . . . Does that sound familiar? It describes the world in which we live. People enter the marriage relationship for many reasons. When someone truly loves, she will put her spouse or family first at all times, no matter the costs. She will love until it hurts; she loves hard. Love is both naive and selfless; love is not self-seeking. Why then do individuals in marriages get fixated on having their own way in every situation? Ask yourself this question, "Am I that person in my marriage?" Also, there is an underlying mentality at play here: to protect one's property or assets "just in case." In today's culture, the word *pre-*

nuptial is a rather common one. Persons show a great sense of devotion to the one they love and intend on marrying, yet there is much self-seeking involved. Simply put, what's mine is mine, and what's yours is mine. Getting married with a self-seeking mentality or with negative motives can put a real strain on the marriage. There will always be that unspoken feeling or thought that neither person wants to tackle, in fear that the words may not come out right. It would appear that many relationships these days are often based on the "what's in it for me?" mind-set. The sanctity and sacredness of marriage has been lost in a Hollywood-driven world and is tainted with lust and fantasies. A marriage must be fashioned from a mutual and a loving foundation sanctioned by God without any strings attached or without wrong motives and manipulation. When two have truly become one, then there will be an environment that fosters trust and team building, where words such as *I, me, my,* and *mine* only complement words such as *ours, we,* and *us.* It is safe to say that one who enters a marriage relationship with a self-seeking attitude struggles with trust. In fact, it is clear that she has never truly learned what it means to trust. Love's desire at all times is to see each other at their very best. One must recognize the personal need for change and make the necessary steps to do so for the health of the marriage.

Love Is *Not* Easily Angered; It Keeps *No* Record of Wrong

It takes nothing these days to see how angry people really are around us and in our world at large. Persons will find various reasons to protest as to why they have the right to be angry. Rightfully so, many do have reasons to be angry, but to some degree, don't we all? If we look all around us, we can see a stalemated economy, wars, disasters of great proportions, brokenness of all sorts, and the list goes on. Likewise, a marriage relationship is not immune to problems and can be full of misunderstandings. However, it is our incumbent response that determines the outcome of every disagreement. Couples are responsible to seek out healthy and effective ways when dealing with conflicts. Communication is made next to impossible when there is constant anger involved. Who wants to be around an angry person, much more to be in conversation with one? Love is not easily angered. An angry person dampens the room and muzzles the possibilities for conversations. The only thing anger initiates is more anger. Do not entertain anger—an angry spirit loves companionship. Being combative only fuels the fire. It is not a logical solution to fight fire with fire. An angry person will often go out of the way to frustrate another. Do you ever notice that in the attempt to start a civilized discussion with your partner, the moment they get angry, all that's going through your head are thoughts and emotions to run, hide, cover your ears, ignore every word, answer everything with yeses and nos, or worst, join the anger party? Your response has the ability to defuse or to ignite an already-tense situation. You can choose to either win your spouse with your words or risk losing him or her. Always intentionally consider each word before speaking. A soft and gentle word may be the winning ingredient to that conversation. Be constructive and edifying, not destructive. Don't allow your marriage to be drawn into that deadly cycle. Once you are there, it is very difficult to retreat or move to a place of normalcy.

Love keeps no record of wrongs, nor does it set out to do evil, and neither should we. Love sets out to heal permanently. Hurting people hurts others, even the ones they love. Every moment you or your spouse chooses to hold on to past issues is a missed opportunity to experience lost happiness. Prolonged anger and unforgiveness eat away at the foundation of a marriage. What may appear externally as a love relationship will soon enough begin to expose cracks in the marriage, if parties don't seek the necessary guidance or help required. It's a very frightening place when married couples begin living their lives day by day like two ships passing by each other in the night. When two people stop communicating or responding about the things they once viewed as important, they need to begin to take stock of their marriage. Love and forgiveness go hand in hand.

Remembering Your Vows

There is quite a buildup of emotions that every couple faces as they anticipate the big day. It can be overwhelming at times with the reality of the wedding day approaching. There's so much to consider and accomplish, with very little time for preparation. This is why most couples simply miss the significance of the two most important words they will ever have to say on their wedding day: "I do." These two words, as elementary as they appear, are two of the foundational pillars that will determine the success or the demise of a marriage. After the honeymoon has ended and the realities of life have kicked in, those two words are often put to the test. Each person now has to demonstrate their commitment, which automatically requires action. You cannot be a bystander; you must be an active participant. "I do'" doesn't have to end posthoneymoon. In fact, despite all the good and the bad that is packaged in the marriage relationship, most flourishing marriages today consider the honeymoon as everyday practical living and not just an event as such. The wedding day and everything that happens leading up to that day are merely events. The marriage begins swiftly after the vows are made.

We live in a world where words are just words and nothing more. Did you know there is life and death wrapped up in the words we speak (Proverbs 18:21)? In fact, in ancient times as we know it, a man's word was all he had that protected his character. If he made a promise or a verbal contract with his neighbor, he had to fulfill it or this could mean death to him, his livestock, or his family. Therefore, it was in his best interest to fulfill his vows as he was held accountable for every word he spoke. He would have been bound by it and would even have died for it. What makes today's culture any different? Fewer people today understand what it means to be accountable. Accountability is replaced by entitlement! People say a lot of things they do not mean or even know the meaning thereof. Similarly, people today get into marriages with the very same attitude. The words "I do" are subjective in today's world. Very few seem to give credence to the thought of covenant. The term "till death do us part" has lost its relevance and meaning in today's culture in exchange for self-gratification. Most people use the words "I do" to suit their own convenience. These are some reasons as to why people don't live up to their vows:

- *I do* until I'm tired of you.
- *I do* until you don't agree with me.
- *I do* until the money runs out.

- *I do* until the kids are grown.
- *I do* until someone better (younger, more attractive, etc.) comes along.
- *I do* until I no longer want to be married because it's not convenient anymore.
- *I do* until I discover your flaws.
- *I do* until I can no longer forgive you.

"I do" does not mean "Maybe," "Perhaps," "Depends," "Sort of," "We'll see," or "Let me think about it." Once you have uttered the words "I do," you have automatically entered in a verbal and a spiritual contract with your spouse. Much like a legally binding contract that carries the weight of words that are taken seriously by the parties involved. Why then shouldn't your marriage be given the same respect or much greater? Your covenant/vows are forever, until death. As scary as that sounds, it is doable.

Remembering your vows takes two. The responsibility cannot rely solely on one person. The person working the hardest in this or any other areas in the marriage will experience frustration and burn-out. This is a common occurrence and one of the number one complaints couples have. However, does this mean the one who is trying the hardest in this area of the relationship loves more than the one who seems to not be trying at all? Not necessarily so. Yet the one who is accused of not trying may argue that he/she shows love differently. While that might be true, it is not recommended that this behavior be justified. Whenever an excuse is given for a behavioral pattern, it fuels that person's action, it causes complacency, and it empowers the continued behaviors that are all recipes for much-greater problems in the future. The longevity of your marriage lies in the remembrance of your wedding vows. Not recalling or regurgitating on the importance thereof proves to be the death of most marriages today. The vows are much like needed energy or air, which offers vitally to the body. On any given day, have you ever forgotten to breathe? Can you imagine what that picture actually looks like? Do not suffocate your marriage by relinquishing your vows. Ever so often, both partners should use their vows to remind themselves, in the good or the not-so-good times, how much they truly love each other. Do not take the moments of your former years for granted. Instead, build on them. Those are the years that are archived in your minds that remind you of the triumphs you've had that have caused you to endure this far. Always remember, you can do all things through Christ, who gives you strength (Philippians 4:13).

What Is Your Vision for Your Marriage?

Do you have a plan for your marriage? Have you and your partner ever taken some time to sit down and pen out what it is you both desire and what the future of your marriage should look like? When you write something down such as a recipe, a direction to a destination, a personal goal, or merely a thought for the next big idea that could change your life forever, doesn't it make the journey or the impossibilities that much clearer? While you are not able to predict all the events of your future, it helps when you have a guide or a road map of some sort. The same is true when you have made a declaration and a vision for your marriage. Too often, individuals enter into the marriage relationship blindly, with no concept of their future life. Because they never started off as such, they figure they will just play things by ear. Those are some of the relationships that fizzle out after a few years. They start up with more fiery passion than you can find in a champagne bottle that only lasts for a brief moment in time. Where there is no vision, the people perish (Proverbs 29:18).

It is very easy to confuse wishful thinking with vision. Wishful thinking is based on a flimsy fantasy—it bears no weight—whereas vision is based on godly principles that are relevant and timeless. So many people invest an enormous amount of time, energy, money, emotions, and thought into a single day—the wedding day. For all those components to come together, it takes teamwork and plenty of compromise. Likewise, wouldn't it be as equally important to invest the same amount of effort into the vision for your relationship? At some point leading up to the wedding day, it would be in your best interest as a couple to sit down and talk about your hopes and your ns. After the wedding day has come and gone, it would be a good time to revisit what you've discussed for your future. Here are some examples of goals and visions for a marriage:

- Individual aspirations (career, spirituality, etc.)
- Living arrangements (owning a home or renting)
- Starting a family
- Finances
- Career

Another crucial element of having a vision for your marriage is making sure the vision is the same one between the two of you. It isn't enough to simply have a vision—that is, a vision of your own, separate from your spouse! This isn't to say that you cannot have different gifts. In fact, this can greatly complement the marriage. Just make sure you both pursue a vision that converges between yourself and your spouse. Are you both participants of this vision?

Later on in the book, we will get into further detail about important things to consider, including visions and goals, before entering a marriage covenant.

It is God's heart for marriages to succeed and be fruitful. Therefore, it is vitally important that your vision is aligned with God's will. Both parties must desire what God desires. In order to know what God desires, first, you both must know his original intent for marriage. This is found in the heart of scripture. From the beginning, God's purpose for humanity was to reflect his own nature through us. Man and woman became one. There are three main ingredients that God intended to solidify the vision of a marriage.

The Three *C*s

- Communion—intimate fellowship
- Covenant—commitment between man and woman or between God and man (continuity)
- Completion—when two become one

Communion

Before the inception of Adam, God's design was to have intimate fellowship between himself (Father, Son, and Holy Spirit) and creation. God wanted to reflect his divine nature through humanity. It is no wonder that he established the institution of marriage. Marriage also personifies the relationship between Christ and his bride—the church. There is no marriage where there is no love. Communion in a marriage requires an exchange of love. God's intent for communion was to express love. This cannot be done without relationship. We are a rough copy of who he is as we are created in his image. To fully understand what it means to have intimate fellowship in a marriage, both parties must understand their origin, which is found only in the Creator himself.

Covenant

In today's culture, the word *covenant* has simply lost its meaning. We live in a throwaway society. When something doesn't work, rather than trying to find a solution to fix it, we just throw it away. This is also the case with relationships. Most individuals stay in a relationship for as long as it is convenient. Covenant, like old furniture, has become disposable—both consciously and subconsciously. Covenant in itself is defined by permanence. God honors covenant as it reflects his eternal nature. Covenant requires commitment and continuity in marriage.

Completion

Do you feel complete? What does this really look like? Innately, in all of us, there is a genuine desire for companionship. Loneliness can plague the life of an individual like a cancer if the void for a companion is not filled. Most people live their lives with a temporary approach of what companionship means because it has been ingrained in our culture as such. Subsequently, some may never experience true companionship. God saw that Adam was alone, and out of that void, he created a woman for him. God's intention for companionship was for the woman to complete and complement the man. The two became one. Their interdependence meant that they needed each other for support for the entirety of their lives.

These three *C*s are fundamental principles that fuel the life of a healthy, God-centered marriage relationship. If your marriage is truly ordained by God and these principles are lived out, it will be built on a solid foundation. Why? Communion ensures that the door of communication stays open. Covenant speaks to the reciprocal promise made by each other and solidifies trust. Completion brings out the best in each person. It also enables the discovery of one's true identity in the other. Allegorically speaking, the woman in this case is Adam's missing rib. His identity is complete once she enters his life.

Assignment:

What are some of the characteristics of your ideal spouse?

_____

_____

_____

What is the Vision for your marriage?

_____

_____

_____

Chapter 2

Space Makes Waste

If space were the solution to fixing the missing link for a broken chain, some chain that would be. A tire that's losing air doesn't need more space; it requires that all space be permanently sealed. There are many things in life that require space—the marriage relationship is not one of them. Space in a marriage is a definitive equation for more potential problems. It is the perfect storm combination, if you may. If both parties cannot resolve their issues while being together, what is the likelihood of them doing so while being apart? Space makes waste, especially when there is no real accountability structure in place during this time apart. Persons are left vulnerable and are exposed, which may complicate things even further. Their weaknesses begin to surface, and they are left abandoned to fall into temptations. No one is above temptation! Couples should bear in mind that they are no longer in a dating situation but rather a marriage! While disagreements will come and growing pains are inevitable, space is never the solution. It is appropriate in these difficult moments that couples look beyond themselves and seek the necessary counseling that brings perspective. Continued counseling is essential as a means of support and guidance. Godly counseling is needed as the driving force and the compass that will lead to healing and reconciliation. No one person needs counseling more than the other. Once counseling is needed, it applies to both parties. Couples should perhaps explore group sessions as well as individual sessions. This may cause shocking revelations in the process, which are crucial in finding out the real root of the existing problems. Much like employment, whenever there is an opening or a space, it is an indication for vacancy. Subsequently, something or someone will endeavor to fill that space.

A 2011 study done at Laval University that was published by the *Toronto Star* is yet another attack on the institution of marriage. As if there aren't enough studies out there that are contrary to the practices and values of marriage, this study suggests this: "Could sleep divorce be the answer to insomnia or restless slumber? We sleep better when we sleep alone." It went on to say, "Save your marriage with sleep divorce."

The "Cave"

Further to this point, it is culturally acceptable in North American culture today for men to have what is considered a "man cave." This is where the man isolates himself from his wife and family as a means of escape. As if an escape is needed from marriage. Some women are OK with this behavior. In fact, some women even have a "woman cave." These areas of the home are off-limits for the other spouse. They serve as a metaphorical pacifier to relieve tension or stress. Truth be told, it is a cop-out approach to dealing with the hard issues of marriage, such as communication, family interaction, etc. Breathe. Certainly this will hit a nerve for many, but don't shred these pages just yet. This is not a blanket statement; however, it's worthy of consideration because this innocent act of blowing off some steam or just hangin' with the guys/girls too easily ends up creating a wedge over time. It is insidious because on the surface, it appears totally harmless. Like all things, moderation is the key. When "man cave" or "woman cave" becomes a lifestyle, it has the potential to isolate couples and pull them apart. It is important that couples learn how to cope with stressful situations that do not require isolation. Instead, couples would benefit much more in finding common ground in the activities they share. Sadly, as time rolls by in the relationship, especially after marriage, couples drift apart. Marriage becomes a drag and uninteresting due to the stress of bills, work life, children, and the daily monotonous routines. Think back to the very beginning of your relationship. What did you share in common?

- Did you go for long walks on the beach or at the park?
- Did you enjoy playing board games?
- Did you enjoy the arts?
- Did you watch a movie?
- Did you volunteer in the community?
- Did you work out?
- Did you connect with other couples?
- Did you take a vacation together?

It is important for couples to not lose sight of what they have in common. Take some time to sit down and communicate about what you both enjoy and find ways to incorporate it into your daily lives. Your partner should never become your roommate. Otherwise, you run the risk of living separate lives under the same roof. Your marriage is worth fighting for. The question is, what is God's heart on the matter? Personal prayer time quiets our heart and emotions and leads us to act rationally in these moments of uncertainty.

Taking time apart in attempt to restore the marriage often seems like a quick fix. The truth is, time apart only causes *more* division. Your problems will be right there waiting for you when you get back—and be even magnified. This scenario is reminiscent of the prescription drugs flaunted daily on television. Consider the parody below illustrating this thought:

> *Drug: Time Fx*
> *Take this medication in times of marital distress.*
> *Side effects may include small bursts of youthful lust, momentary episodes of liberation followed by deep feelings of emptiness, bouts of sadness, hardening of the heart, swelling of the ego, increase in pride levels, emotional constipation followed by verbal diarrhea, height-*

*ened expectations, decline of intimacy, and possible
death of the marriage.*

*Talk to your pastor or spiritual physician before
taking this treatment.*

As most prescription drugs do, the Time Fx drug begins to lack
appeal as you read the small print on the side effects. In reality, time
may seem to offer a therapeutic approach to restore a suffering marriage, but in the long run, the side effects outweigh the initial relief.

Here are some reasons why couples consider taking space:

There Is No Connection

Two cannot walk together unless they agree in spirit. True connection begins in the spirit. While there are different levels of connection mentally, emotionally, and physically, the spiritual connection is the most vital connection of them all. Why? It allows you to
see the person for who they truly are. If the relationship lacks the
spiritual connection, by default, the other levels of connection will
suffer. None of the other levels are a real foundation; they are mere
components, at best. Having a spiritual connection is a powerful
thing in a relationship because when life happens, the couple is no
longer relying on their own emotional, physical, or mental strength
but on God's. When couples understand this principle, they avoid
the common pitfalls of marriages. Having said this, spiritual connection must be nurtured. Many couples feel that taking space from
each other can be therapeutic to their relationship. For some, this
may seem to be the only option.

However, when someone says "Perhaps we need to take some
space," it's often one of the first signs of trouble in the marriage.
Although there is usually one person (if not both) who feels this way,
this curveball can be avoided if both parties are willing to swallow
their pride and seek out the necessary counseling. In the midst of
counseling, there are still simple and practical behaviors that facili-
tate the marriage connection. Bear in mind, nothing happens over-

night. For instance, a marriage loses its youthfulness when individuals become too comfortable. They take each other for granted and no longer respond in the sweet and cute ways they did before. They no longer laugh at each other's stupid jokes, tickle each other, make funny faces, share inside jokes, text cutesy messages to each other, blow kisses, or share smiles, just to name a few. Although marriage is not child's play, there should be room or flexibility for lightheartedness. This helps keep the flame lit in the marriage. However, when things are taken too seriously, the novelty of it all gets lost. At this point, there is no room to recapture the silly and childish things that once were enjoyed. Maintaining connection is vital. It's the momentum needed for a thriving relationship or marriage. Couples don't necessarily need to look for new things or ways to freshen things up. Instead, they just need to remember the things that brought them joy at first glance. Though things and times have changed, your love for each other shouldn't. The only change needed is growth and maturity.

Appreciation is a key element of the marriage relationship that is worth exploring. Your partner desires genuine support throughout the life of the marriage. It should not feel like a chore. It must be intentional and honest, without manipulation. Many marriages today lack intentionality. It does no good pretending to support or appreciate your partner based on guilt or coercion. Such an attempt is an unhealthy approach. It solves nothing but rather creates other prolonged issues. If your partner says "Why don't you ever support or appreciate me like you used to?" take that as a 911 call for help. It must not be ignored. It requires your urgent effort and attention. Your response always determines the outcome. In the case of the male partner, he may not know how to actually respond to his wife in this situation. A hug or a genuine smile may show the emotional response needed. Oftentimes, these gestures are better than nothing at all. The deer-in-headlights look is not the correct response; neither is closing up and shutting down. Each person may respond differently, given their temperament and maturity. In the end, the person crying out for help needs to know their partner has their best interest at heart. Make a special effort to get to know your spouse's emotional cues. Learning to work together while lifting each other up in difficult moments is essential.

Someone Changed

Quite often in marriages, you hear couples say "He has changed" or "She has changed." In this situation, no one will be the first to admit that they have changed. Instead, there is always the "blame-game syndrome." Blaming, simply put, intensifies the existing problems. The only time a partner admits to changing is when he subconsciously finds himself blaming her for causing him to change. No one can cause another to change against his/her will. Nonetheless, change is a choice based on variables or circumstances that are imposed. Choosing to change is a choice. The opposite is just as true. Change is more of a mind-set that is reflected through one's behavior or attitude in a relationship or life. Furthermore, it must be noted that when a partner has changed or has become an unrecognizable person in the marriage relationship, inevitably the other party may experience change as well. This is not uncommon. As a result, a battlefield is created, and peace is only but a distant thought. Expect insults and name-calling to increase. Because of these types of attacks, the marriage has become something to survive rather than something to enjoy. Don't fight fire with fire. Sometimes when love grows cold, nothing you will ever say or do will be the right to respark the flame. It is a natural inclination in wanting to restore what was lost, to instinctively try to buy the other person's love. Trying to buy the love of another will be the most expensive and risky purchase you will ever make. Don't do it. Time is the master of it all. It is impossible to rush time or even delay it. Practice patience and prayer. You cannot change anyone but yourself. These reactions are a result of hurt. To stop the cycle of hurt, someone needs to take the high road and choose to submit their will under the others'. This approach is counterintuitive to pop culture. But it works. This is a true demonstration of what love is. When both parties take this approach, it is that much more powerful. The marriage is bound to thrive because they are both active participants. On the flip side, if both persons are experiencing hurt and are acting out of hurt, the relationship is bound to fail. Hurting people hurts others, even the ones they love.

Sex Life Sucks

The sex life is always one of the first areas of a marriage to suffer casualties. Significant repair may be needed when the sex life is dried up. Couples should endeavor to form unbreakable bonds throughout their marriage relationship. Sex is a sacred bond that must be preserved at all costs or it will cost you! Withholding from intimacy is one of the common traps in a marriage. Do not fall into it because its fall may break your marriage in ways that can never be repaired but by the grace and mercies of God. Much like having a pet, if you fail to care for and feed that pet, it will run away, perhaps to your neighbor or the streets, until it finds food. The same can be said in a marriage when sex is withheld. However, this example does not justify cheating. It is *not* a free ticket for unfaithfulness. The sex life can suck in a marriage when couples fail to live a balanced life. For instance, the decision to start a family may be yet the most important one in a marriage. Many find this decision to be rewarding. It is a couple's duty to ensure that once children are a part of the equation, their sex life remains intact. Children often pose new challenges. They demand time and a lot of affection. Both parties have to ensure that while they are allotting time and affection toward their child/children, they schedule time for each other as well. While scheduling may not seem like an easy task at first, the efforts will surely pay off over time in the relationship. Another factor that may hinder intimacy in a relationship could result from a job or career. The busyness of life can cause parties to overlook each other or pending matters of the heart that are of great importance. Whenever that happens, it often creates loopholes in the marriage. Let's not forget, throughout all busyness of life, the need for love and affection still exists. Sex is vital in a marriage:

- It relieves stress.
- It calms and comforts the emotions.
- It tightens the bonds of intimacy.
- It opens the door of communication.

Remember when you first met? Your passion burned for each other uncontrollably. At that point, life was blissful as you gazed into each other's eyes for hours unending. The sex was great, and nothing could go wrong. These should not remain distant memories but instead a lifestyle. If you can perceive it, then reach for it and live it. Take the necessary time that is needed to strengthen and grow this area in your marriage. It is one of the components that glue the relationship. Sexual intimacy was created by God for the marital pleasure and enjoyment. It is important that couples guard and preserve it so that it will not be stifled by the cares and stresses of life. Couples can avoid the expenses of therapy if only they discover this.

You Cannot Change Your Partner

Your partner is not *a reconstruction project.*

If you were to be honest with yourself and ask yourself the question "How many times have you tried to change someone you thought you knew?" more often than not, you find that you end up frustrating yourself in the process. True or false? Would you agree that this has caused you more anxiety, countless tears as you cried yourself to sleep, increased hopelessness, not to mention the devastation of repeatedly failed expectations?

Only God has the power to change a person. What would compel you to pursue a relationship with someone whose character flaws cause you to compromise your values and standards? Much like a business venture, it is not advisable to enter a partnership with someone who clearly does not share the same goals and values as you. From the inception of the relationship, both parties must demonstrate a willingness to not just coexist but align their personal ideals in order to complement each other. *Never* assume that by entering this relationship, your spouse will change. The premise of your relationship should be based on unconditional love for your partner, not selfish ideals. Because of selfish ideals, many people find themselves in toxic relationships where they have to conjure up ways to manipulatively con their partner into becoming something or someone they're not. At this point, this only brings out the worse in each other. Instead of putting all your energy into changing your partner, why not direct that constructive energy into becoming your best self? When both individuals understand this principle without very much effort, they subconsciously will make their best contribution to the well-being of the relationship as a result.

Toxic relationships are a by-product of counterfeits. An example of such would be a victim-villain relationship. The victim is often the person who is being forced to conform, and the villain is the person who is enforcing their will upon the other. At any given time, the roles have a way of flip-flopping. This may result in further bitterness, strife, and misunderstandings, which open the door for greater future problems. The onus is on both parties in this case; they must take active responsibility for their own choices and actions. This works both ways, whether you consider yourself the victim or not. Say you meet someone and warning bells start to go off that the person is wrong for you by devaluing you or your standards; if you willingly choose to ignore the red flags and force yourself to stay in the relationship for the sake of making it work, you are only deceiving yourself. From the inception, if you feel that something is wrong about your partner, then it probably is.

How do you know when the person you are with is truly being genuine about who they are? It is very difficult to know who a person really is in the early stages of courting. In fact, it is through marrying your spouse and living together that you will truly know who you're with. One must be prepared for that fact. These are three practical guidelines to consider before marriage:

- ✓ Listen to your gut feeling as well as trusted loved ones in your life, and don't second-guess it; investigate it (gut feeling = God feeling).
- ✓ Educate yourself on what it means to be street-smart when entering a relationship. Learn to identify red flags.
- ✓ Seek premarital counseling to assess personality traits, which should provide insight on compatibility.

Before you scrap this chapter, take a moment to pause and introspectively consider this. If you are willing to let someone tear you down, this is characterized as false humility. It is deception and naivety. One must learn how to love oneself before one can love someone else. The golden rule sets the standard: treat others as you would have them treat *you*. You are part of that equation, and when you cut yourself out of it, you're eluding yourself. Don't compromise who you are for someone else. Don't lose yourself and your soul in the process. You are not your own—you are God's child. The spirit within you requires stewardship. If you are willing to risk your values and self-worth for the temporary relief of having that person in your life when you know in your spirit that they will break you down, you have already committed a crime against yourself and your Creator. You are, in fact, being selfish and precarious, and you are only hurting yourself. Do not sacrifice your values for instant gratification that will cost you much trauma later on.

You have intrinsic value. You are priceless. You are not to be violated. You were fearfully and wonderfully made by a Creator who loves you to death (literally) and thinks the world of you. Why should you allow anyone else to treat you differently? When you concede this, you, by default, have already committed idolatry; you have elevated this other person to the place of God. This scenario is not only vastly skewed, but it's unhealthy and downright fatal to your spiritual being. Whether you subscribe to a Christian worldview or not, this system is doomed to fail. Don't shortchange yourself. To be unevenly yoked is self-depicted in its very terminology; the yoke of the other person will weigh you down and cause you to fall and crumble. What does the Bible mean when it talks about the uneven yoke? The load is meant to be distributed evenly between two people. God's plan for relationship is encrypted in this illustration (2 Corinthians 6:14).

The key to avoid expecting to change a person is recognizing the cues in their character traits from the very beginning. Ask yourself, do I truly like this person just the way they are? There is a stark difference between partnership and babysitting. We are not called to be spousal babysitters! This analogy depicts the problem explicitly. A babysitter is someone who is hired on to exercise authority over the well-being of another person. Right away in that scenario, we have a problem; one person assumes responsibility over the other. It's imperative that we identify the roles of each party in a relationship. A relationship is a partnership, not a day care. Both parties are equally held accountable for their actions toward each other. They function as a team, not a dictatorship. This is often why, in suffering relationships, one of the parties feels they are being controlled or manipulated. There is a sense of inequality and confusion about their roles. This is catastrophic to the relationship; it catapults each person out of equilibrium and picks up momentum over time until the relationship is devastated. When you marry someone, you marry their baggage. One must be prepared for this fact. Before marriage, you may not be able to resolve all your stuff or issues. Remember to demonstrate the same grace toward the other person as you would like in return. Keep in mind that neither of you are marrying a perfect person. It's important that both spouses take the time to work on themselves. Personal development is crucial to a healthy marriage. Both spouses should encourage each other to work on their own personal issues first, rather than focusing on the other person's faults or baggage.

Addressing Symptoms VS Root

We live in a Band-Aid society. People are constantly looking for a quick-fix solution to their problems. In most cases, these are temporary solutions that do not deal with the cause/root of their problems. Many marriages suffer at the mercy of this mentality. We would live in a utopian world if all our marital issues would dissolve at the snap of a finger. Marriage takes work. In fact, it is a full-time responsibility.

Doctors and psychiatrists alike are quick to administer medication for just about everything. While medications are helpful for some things, the side effects they cause could be more damaging than expected. Have you seen the commercials on TV that offer arthritis pain relief? They will sound something like this: "Do you suffer from horrible, crippling arthritis pain? Well, we finally found the solution that you've been looking for! You can be pain-free and get your life back by taking this product. However, side effects may include nausea, dry mouth, indigestion, liver disease, congestive heart failure, blindness, internal bleeding, and possible death. Consult your physician before taking this product." As is painfully evident, the side effects greatly outweigh the initial illness. This analogy reflects the common problem in marriages—we often mask the problem with "drugs," suppressing the real issues, which, in turn, cause other vital organs to deteriorate. Most times, all that is required are practical steps that are often overlooked by couples.

These steps may include:

- Counseling (group and individual)
- Actively listening to each other—paying attention and being empathetic to what the other is saying
- Discerning when to speak—timing is everything
- Exposing your hurts—being intentional without manipulation
- Exercising patience and grace with each other—fostering a caring environment
- Starting off by being honest with each other—covering up one's faults will not solve anything
- Forgiving each other—without holding grudges or being judgmental

Following these steps will expose the root of your marital problems. Only by addressing the root can a true healing process begin.

The chart below outlines common symptoms that are often mistaken for roots in the marriage relationship. Couples tend to blame one or more of these things as they try to come to terms with their marital issues. This would be a good time to take a moment with your spouse to see which of these you can relate with, particularly the subject matter in the "Symptoms" column. In your evaluation, see if you come up with the same root cause as below. Your conclusion may surprise you as you talk through this exercise with your spouse.

Symptom	Root
Addiction	Selfishness, pride, and fear
Financial problems	Greed, selfishness, pride, and disrespect
Infidelity	Selfishness, disrespect, and pride
Lack of appreciation	Selfishness and disrespect
Intimacy issues	Pride and selfishness
Power struggle	Pride/ego and selfishness
Bad communication / lack thereof	Pride and selfishness

Avoiding a problem does not negate its existence. Couples often refuse to talk about resurfacing issues because they hope it will just deal with itself and go away. Not so. The root of these symptoms or problems can be simply diagnosed through communication. It is communication that opens the door to dealing with core issues, which leads to problem solving. In the chart above, there are three resurfacing roots: pride, selfishness, and disrespect. These three roots are central themes to this book. They can relate to just about any given issue that rises in a marriage. They are the most insidious roots yet the most overlooked. By nature, roots are hidden. They existed even before the marriage. Individuals enter into marriage with pre-existing behavioral issues, not seeing the need for change. In their minds, they are thinking, *This is how I've always done it. I don't see the need to change.* With this mentality, your marriage has failed even before it has begun. These three roots can also apply to any given situation in one's life, not just the marital relationship. Yet there is hope. Marriages today don't need to end in divorce. If couples would learn to realistically tackle these three predominant roots, marriages would thrive. This does not negate that problems will arise; however, identifying and eradicating these roots will lead to healing and foster a healthy relationship. It is important to remember that these roots do not surface in any particular order, yet they comfortably coexist. Where there is one, the other two will inevitably follow.

Let's examine the characteristics of pride, selfishness, and disrespect:

Pride

- is egotistic, having a counterfeit perception of one's self
- doesn't admit to or see faults in one's self or lacks perspective
- creates a false sense of security
- will always see the wrong in others first
- lacks humility and will not submit
- always wants to win
- is stubborn in nature and unwilling to compromise
- is always driven by wrong motives

Selfishness

- only sees or thinks about oneself—"number one"
- lacks concern for the best interest of others
- acts out of emotional response as opposed to morals
- gains at the expense of others
- is unwilling to make sacrifices
- doesn't listen to others' perspective and is unwilling to take counsel

Disrespect

- defiles the character of others and causes others to act out of character
- shows no remorse for wrong actions
- is rude, blunt, insensitive, violent, and belligerent/coldhearted
- is quick to cast judgment
- is condescending
- is irrational
- does not value the opinions of others
- is quick to walk away or dismissive
- lacks honor

It is very easy for couples to overlook these characteristics. It is imperative that they identify these and deal with them. You can come out strong when your root and foundation is right. God's word contains the blueprint for marriage and should be used as such. Stop trying to patch your relationship month after month, year after year, and face the root issues and deal with them head-on. Failing to admit there is a problem only perpetuates it. It is only a matter of time before the roots choke out the relationship. Using an agricultural analogy, if the seed is right, then the root will be right, resulting in good fruit. In the context of marriage, your end is not as important as your beginning. One must be rooted and grounded in love, according to the apostle Paul in Ephesians 3:17. Your love for your partner should triumph over bad roots, because true love never fails (1 Corinthians 13:8). Why? Because love contains all the necessary nutrients to strengthen the foundation of the marriage. There must be love in the seed and love in the fruit. There cannot be fruit before root, and unfortunately, people enter the marriage relationship hoping for fruitfulness without addressing the preexisting roots. What anchors you? What are the foundations that you are hoping to build on? These are vital and must be evaluated before entering a relationship. For example, if you start off selfish, the fruit of your marriage will reflect that. All of us, to some degree, struggle in all three root areas. Whether you struggle with one or all three of these roots, they will ultimately have an impact on your marriage. Deal with it now, not later.

Emphasizing on Minor Details while Failing at Major Issues

In this segment, we are introducing two reconstructed words—*agreegament* and *disagreegament'*—in order to further emphasize the point of dealing with symptoms. Unknowingly, most married couples build fortresses of excuses. They justify their behavior and refuse help as they barricade themselves in their protective lair. They build walls that are so high that no one can get over them. At this point, they become unreachable. They fail to deal with the elephant in the room. Instead, they find more and more reasons to build their walls higher. They waste energy emphasizing on minor things while neglecting the major issues.

While communication is strongly encouraged, the method used is that much more important. Here are two methods that we have identified in our own marriage, which we have coined *agreegament* and *disagreegament* for lack of adjectives.

Agreegament (ah-gree-gah-mint): when two parties are engaged in a discussion and appear to be disagreeing when, in fact, they are both saying the exact same thing, but from two different perspectives.

**Example: Maddie says the cup is half full. Sean says it is half empty. They are both basically saying the same thing but expressing it in different terms. (Putting aside all philosophical associations, this example is being used for illustrative purposes only.)

Disagreegament (dis-ah-gree-gah-mint): when two parties are engaged in a discussion and disagree on a given topic but both parties *respectfully* compromise and choose to agree to disagree on the more logical conclusion.

**Example: Carmen claims that the color of the car is simply green. Margaret says it is bluish green. After some playful debate concerning color blindness, they conclude that it is definitely a greenish hue, but they both reserve their original views.

When either methods of communication occur, couples are encouraged to identify them. This eliminates the element of competition, and both parties win. Conversation in a marriage is not a competition. In order for a healthy relationship to thrive, dialogues should be viewed as building blocks to edify the marriage, rather than weapons.

Just Listen

Another key method of communication is the ability to *just* listen. It's a real art sometimes to just sit back quietly and listen to your spouse without trying to fix them or the issue. In order to be a great communicator, you need to start by being a good listener. It's important that you listen to your spouse's heart, not just the words that are being spoken. Too often, we are so quick to respond that we haven't allowed ourselves to process what is actually being said. As a result, we lack discernment on how to respond. It can be as simple as offering a hug or holding their hand. In certain cases, that may be all that is required. When we don't listen effectively, we can end up jumping to wrong conclusions, sparking unnecessary arguments, unintentionally hurting our spouse, or causing them to shut down altogether. It is important that we understand the differences in how men and women are wired. In general, women tend to process their emotions verbally, while men process their emotions internally. The environment in which we were raised also plays a factor in how we listen and communicate. Couples need to find ways to be able to understand each other's communication methods. In order for this to happen, it is imperative that you are intentionally listening and present when your spouse is pouring out their heart and soul.

Dynamics in a Marriage Breakdown

There are several components that keep the lifeline of a marriage alive. After the marriage has burned a few years of mileage, couples tend to become either more callous or too comfortable—and trying to do better becomes a thing of the past. It is painful and straining on the marriage if the relationship becomes one-sided. The breakdown of your marriage doesn't just happen overnight. It is important to discern behaviors and patterns and address them from inception before they mature. Couples are often caught off guard when they are not paying attention to signs of a possible breakdown. For instance, in this scenario, Lucas and Cindy have been married for the past fifteen years. Lucas is addicted to pornography, yet he has not been able to be honest with his wife about his problems. This started even prior to the marriage. As a result, Lucas has been unfaithful to his wife on several occasions. They have gone through several counseling sessions as they sought reconciliation. Their issues were so deep that they could not resolve their differences. In this scenario, we see a preexisting habit that resulted in the breakdown of the marriage. This is a very common occurrence in marriages today. When you break exclusivity in marriage, you break the bond. In this section, we will examine three distinct components of a marriage that keep its dynamics intact.

The marriage life should resemble the gospel—forgiveness is central, everything you do is wholehearted, and you always put yourself last. In light of the belief system in pop culture, this approach is counterintuitive. Marriage takes work; it's an assignment. The moment you stop working at it, it will stop working for you. Let's examine these three components.

Slow to forgive vs. forgive fast. It's easy to feel obligated to forgive or entitled to receive forgiveness. That defeats the purpose of forgiveness. When you break down the word *forgiveness*, you notice the words *for* and *give*. *For*: "with the object or purpose of"; *give*: "freely transfer the possession of [something] to [someone]," "hand over to." Forgiveness, as it were, is a free transfer of one's will. There are no strings attached. True forgiveness is never out of obligation. Couples must learn the art of forgiveness. Forgive fast. The longer it is put off, the harder it becomes to forgive. The emotions snowball over time, leaving the door open for anger and resentment to step in. The only competition there should be in a marriage is to be the first to apologize. Though it is never easy to forgive, it doesn't benefit you to hold grudges. What people often miss about forgiveness is that it is releasing not just for the receiver but for the giver as well. Forgiveness is also attached to a plethora of physical and psychological health benefits. Did you know that the act of forgiveness reduces cholesterol, blood pressure, stress, anxiety, and depression? It also reduces the chance of heart attack and improves sleep. If forgiveness can affect us at a physical level, imagine the wonders it can produce on a spiritual level and for your marriage.

50/50 vs. 100/100. We are taught by our culture today to only put 50 percent of ourselves into a relationship. We are told to act in contingency to our spouse's behavior. We are taught this from a very young age. By God's standard, it is a flawed principle. Clearly, it is not working, as is reflected in the staggering divorce rate at almost 50 percent within the first five years of marriages in North America. Fifty-fifty is a haphazard approach to marriage. Let's take an athlete for instance. It is not practical for an athlete to put half their effort into training. No. An athlete's approach to training is always 100 percent commitment, and the end result reflects that. In order to build stamina, endurance, and skill, the athlete must put their whole heart into it. Marriage is very similar in the sense that it requires a wholehearted approach in order to thrive. Someone who enters the marriage with a fifty-fifty mind-set is setting themselves up for mediocrity. It is like going through the motions without putting your passion into it. This is an escapist mentality, due to the fact that we live in an untrusting culture. We have a subconscious stigma of fear that if we give 100 percent of ourselves, we are setting ourselves up to be hurt. We do not want to be vulnerable. It is much like signing a prenuptial agreement: if things do not go as expected, there is always an out clause. Jesus gave all of himself for the sake of humanity. He held nothing back. Marriage should encompass that same principle: all or nothing at all.

I am first vs. I am second. Choosing to be second in your marriage is one of the greatest benefits you can bring to your marriage. It's the gift that keeps on giving. It is a proactive approach to living. Couples can experience true love when they learn to live out this principle daily. Winning is not the goal in a marriage because it is not a competition. In fact, when the two become one through marriage, they share everything in common because they are one body. Just like in a biological body, every suborganism must coexist with one another as nature intended. If not, there is chaos, and disease takes over. The eye cannot say to the body, "I no longer want to see," or the feet cannot say, "I no longer want to walk." They must work in unison to attain functionality. Being second requires the same principle. Being second says, "I need you to survive, and I will put my own interests aside and put your best interests ahead of my own." What a beautiful picture this paints in a marriage. True love is hidden in the depth of the human soul. By practicing being second, you will begin to discover what true love really means.

Assignment:

Can you identify any bad roots and symptoms in your current or a past relationship?

_____

_____

_____

Are there any "space making" habits you currently practice? If so, what are some ways you can identify that can close the space gap and bring restoration?

_____

_____

_____

Chapter 3

Love—a Concept or Covenant?

Love is not just a concept or an idea; it is a verb. It involves every aspect of yourself—body, mind, and soul. More than a verb, it is a covenant, an unwavering promise. Covenant is not taken lightly by God, as is demonstrated on the pages of scriptures in both the Old and the New Testaments. God instituted covenant to demonstrate his unfailing love to his children. It is the will or desire to give and nurture unconditionally. In our own interpretations, we often see love as somewhat fleeting. Hollywood depicts love as a fairy tale of passion, romance, and fun. Although these are definitely components of love, they aren't the be-all and end-all of love. This perspective of love is very distorted and hollow. It lacks dimension, depth, and longevity. Being in love with the idea of being in love is what people often fantasize about. It is only a reflection of what is depicted on the theater screen. Love is something much more profound. A covenant is a contractual agreement. It is binding and permanent. It requires commitment, which was designed by God from the start to last throughout a lifetime. There are no out clauses or prenups. Suddenly, love loses some of its luster. It almost sounds daunting, as many begin to realize too little too late. Why? Because what they signed up for was never founded on the principles of true love but only a mere idea that has been custom suited to fit their own individual demands. By very definition, love categorically denounces the concept of demand because it is selfless in nature. The nature of love is always, first and foremost, giving. It is the outpouring of oneself into another. When we flirt with the idea of being in love, we get caught up in the bliss of receiving attention and affection from someone. Love is counterintuitive in the sense that it is characterized by giving before receiving. A love covenant requires all the following attributes, as referenced in 1 Corinthians 13:4–7:

- Patience
- Kindness
- Humility
- Respect
- Selflessness
- Gentleness
- Forgiveness
- Goodness
- Truth
- Protection
- Hope
- Perseverance

Love sounds easy but, just like theory, is completely different than practical; it is hard when put to the test. As humans, it is our nature that obscures our vision of what love should look like. We are prone to conceptualize and compartmentalize relationships. We are a product of our past experiences and environments. We have a tainted view of what love is. There are some who see love as a spontaneous outburst that can last for an indefinite amount of time. It is to be enjoyed for the moment, because you will not know when it will end. If your foundation is built on the above principles of a love covenant, it is foolproof because true love *never* fails. On the contrary, when we base a relationship on a conditional ideal, it is a variable that is subject to change at any given time. In fact, it renders the relationship unstable. In today's culture, anything beyond the moment is a scary thought. The ideals of a so-called love relationship are more attractive than the sacrificial components that are required to sustain it. Examples of such ideals may be:

- ✓ He has to be a doctor or a lawyer.
- ✓ She has to be very attractive.
- ✓ He has to be famous.

✓ She can't be overweight.
✓ He has to be at least six feet tall.
✓ She has to love sports.
✓ He cannot work at Walmart or McDonald's.
✓ She cannot make more money than him.
✓ He has to be talented.
✓ She has to be a great cook.
✓ He has to own his own house.
✓ She cannot have previous children.
✓ He cannot be divorced.
✓ She has to be from a certain culture.

These concepts of love are very common. In truth, they are actually misconceptions of what love really is. It is not necessarily a bad thing to have certain standards in place; however, the moment you make them the foundation, you have set yourself up for failure. When these concepts seem to no longer exist in the marriage, dreams crumble and expectations are shattered. Love is perceived as a powerful force outside ourselves that possesses us and we cannot control. This force is a passionate flame that evokes our emotions. True love doesn't hijack us. Love involves our intention. It requires our initiative. It is a constant act of our will that flows out of our desire to uplift that person above ourselves. It is the perpetual submission of self. Think of love as an engine; in order to keep it running, you need to feed it with fuel and maintain it regularly or it will break down. Ideas and concepts are likened to wanting a beautiful car, but you don't want to put the maintenance into it. It will eventually fall apart. Love takes work. It doesn't maintain itself. This is another reason love is often compared to a flame. The fire needs specific environmental conditions to keep burning; otherwise, it will be swiftly snuffed out, as often happens. Concepts are a far cry from how reality may actually play out. Concepts restrict true love, which equals covenant. On the contrary, true love *never* fails because it is not based on the conditions of concepts.

You Are My Best Friend

Interdependency is often frowned upon in our culture. Couples are encouraged to rely on themselves rather than on each other. It is a faux pas for couples to be considered best friends. It is the friends outside your marriage that assume this role. This is a skewed idea of marriage. Doesn't it make sense that the person you intend to share the rest of your life with should know everything about you? Why should your spouse be your third wheel while someone else assumes the role of best friend? Even if you had a best friend prior to marriage, your spouse replaces their role. This is suggesting not that you are to drop this person as your friend but that your spouse now takes priority in your life. A best friend is understood as someone who knows every single intimate detail about you. Your spouse should automatically be promoted to best-friend status, which results in total transparency of both your past and present. A loving spouse who desires to take on the role of best friend will accept you as you are regardless of your past. It's best you are transparent from the start. The true test of a best friend is that they will love and accept you despite your darkest secrets.

The intimate details of your relationship should be strictly kept within the borders of your relationship. This is to maintain the integrity of the marriage. Anyone outside your relationship should only be given information on a need-to-know basis. An outsider is just that. When you allow someone into the boundaries of your marriage, you create the potential for them to put a wedge between you and your spouse. A marriage is a partnership. You are a team. You are one. Finding solutions to your marital issues should be a joint effort. You shouldn't feel obligated to solicit advice outside godly counsel, which should come from a spiritual leader, mentor, or professional counselor. This approach eliminates the potential for receiving biased advice, the spread of gossip, spousal conflicts, breach of confidentiality, and a slew of other potential issues. How would you feel if your spouse relinquished intimate details about you behind your back? Would that create a sense of betrayal? These are common occurrences in marriages today. It is important to guard your relationship and its integrity with your best friend, your spouse. If your spouse is not your best friend, then you become reclusive and secrets begin to develop. Because your spouse is your best friend, it makes conversation easy. Small talks aren't forced, and openness is a natural thing. It creates a safe environment.

A common misconception in our North American culture is the loose approach we have toward respect in any given relationship. The lines of openness and respect become blurred because people feel entitled to abuse them based on their comfort level. Closeness does not equal "I can treat you how I want to treat you." There is still a level of respect that needs to be upheld without the relationship feeling too formal. There needs to be a balance. Mutual respect should always govern a friendship/marriage.

Unity Begins in the Spirit

Having a spiritual connection is just as important as a physical one. In fact, when couples recognize and nurture their spiritual connection that is found through God's Holy Spirit, they create bonds that are unshakable. These bonds of connection are like a threefold cord that causes their unity together to be strengthened. Unity is a spiritual principle that is transcendent. The Bible tells us that a threefold cord cannot easily be broken (Ecclesiastes 4:12). When unity is at its best, it is a beautiful sight. Even without trying, those in its path are moved and inspired and sometimes lit by its flame. The testaments of its flame are best seen in a God-centered marriage.

Couples can experience prevailing unity in their daily lives when they understand that unity begins in the spirit. Unity is a powerful force. Our bodies are mere containers of our spirit man. Our true identity lies deeper than meets the eye. There is disconnection when we try to define our identity outside the spirit of our Creator. The scriptures tell us that we are created in his image. Just as God is triune in divine nature (Father, Son, Holy Spirit), we are a reflection of him as physical beings (spirit, soul, and body). There are very strong parallels between the Triune God and marriage (man, woman, and God). He instituted marriage for a very specific purpose—it paints a beautiful picture of his nature. God's design for the family structure demonstrates the inner workings of his original plan for marriage. As depicted below, the roles of each unit are interdependent yet still equal. In order to function, they must work in unison.

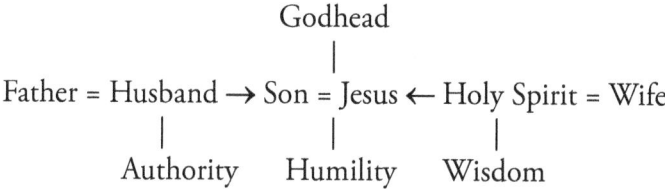

The language of marriage should be *us, we,* and *our,* not *me, mine, your,* and *you.* In communication, we should make a conscious effort to think and speak in these terms. It won't take long for what's on the inside of two people to manifest into the physical. Take for instance when couples say "This is *my* account, and that is *your* account" and "This is *my* money, and that is *your* money." Couples that distinguish their possessions create disunity on every level without even realizing it. In a family structure, *everything* should be shared equally. Possessiveness is a result of mistrust, either from previous relationships or from a lack of understanding of unity. While some believe this is a healthy approach, it's a silent relationship killer. This attitude projects a lack of belief in the longevity or future of your marriage. This false sense of security prevents truth and displays a sense of hopelessness in the union.

Your marriage is your first ministry. It is your responsibility to nurture this gift. Couples often try to separate their callings or visions for ministry. Let's examine the following scenario:

The husband is very musical, and the wife is passionate about missionary work. The husband often sees himself performing for thousands of people at a time in concert as he travels to different parts of the world. This was always his childhood dream. Now that he's married, he struggles with the drastic lifestyle changes. He no longer travels as often as he has had to come to terms with the realities of marriage. Even though he enjoys his married life, he constantly has thoughts of living out this dream one day.

The wife has always envisioned herself travelling to third-world countries to meet the needs of the less fortunate. She has vowed to the Lord that this is something she must do in her lifetime. Yet she also has to come to terms with the realities of being married and the responsibilities thereof.

In the above scenario, there are more similarities to their life visions than there are differences. It is easy for this couple to surmise that they have separate paths in relation to their destiny. However, their paths should not only converge, but they should actually continue on a parallel. Just because they look different in nature doesn't mean they cannot be complementary. In fact, they should be! The goal in a marriage is to create unity. Couples need to build a bridge that connects their paths in life. This creates momentum and a strong support system. Possibilities are endless—they are no longer linear. This discovery motivates each other for excellence. Not knowing each other's purpose can be frustrating at times and may even cause friction. But it is the Spirit of God that teaches you to discern the passions, talents, and aspirations of your spouse and how it uniquely relates to yours. It is a process. Like most processes, this is not instant. It requires trust, patience, and harmony. When you discover your spouse's purpose in life, pursue it together. Your purpose may vary, but you are called *together*. Do not mistake personal dreams of building a legacy with ministry. While one could be the result of another, they are not the same. In ministry, it is more about building someone else and not yourself. In God's eyes, your calling is one and the same. You both will learn with time how important it is to complement each other rather than competing. Scripture tells us, "*If two of you agree on earth concerning anything, it will be done for them by my Heavenly Father*" (Matthew 18:19). Simply put, it only takes two plus the Spirit. You and your spouse, coupled with the Holy Spirit of the Godhead, are an unstoppable force in the pursuit of the destiny of your marriage. This revelation will shape and change the course of your lives together forever.

Your Spouse Is Not Your Enemy

Avoiding confrontation doesn't resolve an issue. By the same token, the freedom to address a conflict or an issue in a relationship should not automatically make you enemies. On the contrary, discussions and diverse points of view in a relationship can be very healthy, provided they are addressed with love and respect. More times than not, it is not *what* has been said but *how* it was said. In a healthy relationship, two people work as a team even when addressing their differences. When two views are put together and not used as weapons against each other, it broadens the perspective. It enables a couple to discover aspects of a matter that would otherwise have not been considered. It is important that couples make an effort to deal with their private issues behind closed doors. Do not air your dirty laundry outside. When you expose sensitive marital issues in public, it opens the door to emotional strife. It's challenging enough to try to resolve an issue between two people, let alone introduce another party. This only complicates things even further, with the potential for biased perspectives.

Couples must remember this one fact: your spouse is not your enemy. The moment you see your spouse as your enemy, you've lost the battle. Don't set yourself up to fail. A failed marriage often rips people apart in devastating ways, not to mention the emotional pains it causes. The rule of thumb in heated conversations should be to think rationally before acting out of your emotions. Too often individuals relive their past through their emotions, which aren't always right. You cannot rely on your emotions alone. Emotions can distort your views of your spouse. A common example is the following:

Sue and Tom just had a heated conversation. She is hurting. She looks across the room and notices that he doesn't look as bothered as she is about what they've just argued about. She used to be in a very destructive relationship in the past, where her ex was emotionally passive-aggressive toward her, especially when they had disagreements. She now equates Tom's apparently nonchalant response to that of her ex-boyfriend.

This is a prime scenario demonstrating how emotions put you on the defensive because they are deceiving. Emotions are not based on absolute truth; they are based on experience—both past and present. Do not allow your past experiences to dictate your present emotional state and responses. This is very dangerous because you will begin to see your partner as an enemy and vice versa. Your disagreements can shape your marriage in a positive or negative way. It is your choice. Every obstacle in your marriage can be used as an opportunity for growth. The obstacle becomes a defeat if you accept it as such. Instead, see the obstacle as a building block to edify your marriage and take it to the next level.

Disagreements will always come; it is how you deal with them that matters. When couples resort to sleeping in separate rooms, they've opened the door to the enemy. Thinking that you are leaving things to blow over is an illusion. In actual fact, they are only being buried and will resurface later on and accumulate interest. Unhealthy roots of bitterness and resentment begin to form. The longer you take to resolve an issue, the harder it becomes over time. It is said that "time is the greatest enemy of hope." Now you've allowed time to stew over a situation, and the problem only seems to magnify due to emotions. Anything that you mismanage will fail. If you mismanage the time that is required to deal with your marital issues, before you know it, it will be too late. These are a few behaviors to watch out for that may indicate you are on the verge of becoming enemies:

- ➢ You are living like roommates.
- ➢ You avoid your spouse.
- ➢ You are constantly irritated by your spouse.
- ➢ You are competitive.
- ➢ You insult or belittle your spouse.
- ➢ You gossip about your spouse.
- ➢ You are driven by hurt emotions.
- ➢ You've lost patience with your spouse.
- ➢ You're no longer gentle but aggressive.
- ➢ Only your perspective matters.
- ➢ There is loss of trust.

➤ You are insensitive toward your spouse.
➤ You no longer believe the best of your spouse.
➤ You don't have your spouse's best interest at heart.
➤ You stop praying for your spouse.
➤ There is loss of hope for the marriage.
➤ You become callous and indifferent.

Don't you know that when attack your spouse, you are hurting yourself? Once you've entered the marriage covenant, you are one unit. God created it as such.

Be encouraged; hang in there—though all hell has broken loose. God's sovereign power and grace are sufficient to keep you both. Whom God has joined, let not man/woman divide. God wants to restore you. Is there anything too hard for God? He is the great Judge, Provider, Restorer, Lover, Comforter, and Friend. Trust in the Lord with all your heart and lean not to your own understanding. In all your ways, acknowledge him and he shall direct your paths (Proverbs 3:5–6)." Perhaps you are reading this and it's just what you needed to hear as you wrestle within yourself. Marriages are under attack, and while hell is trying to pull each one apart, heaven is cheering you on saying: "you can make it!" Don't stop interceding through prayer and never stop believing. Fight, but do it on your knees. Giving up and giving in are *not* options. Your marriage deserves a fighting chance with hope to succeed. The good news is that heaven is on your side. While walking away may seem or feel like a more lucrative thing to do right this second, you could be giving up at the point when you may be right at the edge of a breakthrough. That sucks! There is an upheaval before the storm passes. Perhaps you feel as if you're in the eye of the storm, but follow your spirit, not your emotional heart. The heart is deceitful (Jeremiah 17:19). Make no mistake; when you both get through this, you will be stronger, wiser, and bolder to face life's toughest storms. It will have qualified you as a certified counselor for someone else. More importantly, you will understand why God had you go through it all, at which point you'll be a beacon of light for others to follow. See your victory before it happens.

Assignment:

How do you define love?

_____

_____

_____

How do you deal with disagreements?

_____

_____

_____

Chapter 4

Accountability Partners vs Buddies

Safeguarding the integrity of your relationship is one of the most important things you could ever do for your marriage. Most couples today are of the opinion that they can handle the complexities of their marriage all on their own. This is a myth. If we examine the structural integrity of a building, we can always observe that there are support beams to keep it sturdy and in place. This principle can be applied to accountability partners in marriage. No marriage is immune to problems. It's not a matter of "*if* they will come"; it's a matter of "when."

What does it mean to have an accountability partner? Having accountability partners will provide insight and moral support as tools to keep the marriage grounded. It is important to have accountability partners who share the same spiritual values, someone you look up to. It can be a couple who has accumulated experience in their marriage, perhaps an older couple who has gone before you and can lead the way. It can also be a couple in your age group who can walk alongside you to challenge you on your journey.

Not everyone is qualified to be an accountability partner. It doesn't matter how close you may be with certain individuals or the history you may have with them, be it your family members, best friend, coworkers, or schoolmates, to name a few. In fact, such individuals may provide a biased point of view despite their best intentions. It is too easy for them to become emotionally compromised. They may tell you what you want to hear, as opposed to what you need to hear—what is necessary. There are exceptions to this rule; this is not to diminish close ties with loved ones or friends.

Who are best qualified as accountability partners?
✓ Your family life pastors
✓ Trusted spiritual counselors/mentors
✓ A couple in your church small group

What are the roles of accountability partners?
✓ They pray for you.
✓ They share similar experiences with you.
✓ They are your confidantes.
✓ They mentor you.
✓ They provide unbiased advice and practical help.
✓ They edify and encourage you.
✓ They tell you the truth even when it hurts.
✓ They challenge you to be better.
✓ They help you recognize your blind spots.
✓ They help you focus on what really matters.

A true accountability partner becomes a trusted friend over time. It is very difficult to find such a unique bond. This must not be something you enter into lightly. Always pray and allow the Holy Spirit to lead you to the right partners. Despite the fact that it is very hard for many couples to allow themselves to be vulnerable to someone outside their relationship, it is possible. You may be reading this now and acquainted with what it's like to experience betrayal and hurt. Perhaps it's from a spiritual leader or just a church member and the wound of that hurt still lingers. That makes it ten times harder to trust again. The reality of your hurt, while it is real, can be overcome. Do not allow your hurts to stop you from exploring the possibilities of finding (a) trusted accountability partner(s) for your marriage. The characteristics to look for in an accountability partner are

- ✓ their interaction with others (Do they encourage others, or do they gossip about them?)
- ✓ their marital relationship (Do they respect their spouses, or do they put them down?)
- ✓ their relationship with God (Do they walk according to scriptural principles, or are they hypocrites?)

These are three foundational characteristics that are instrumental to the life of an accountability partner. You cannot follow someone you do not look up to. Neither can you take advice from someone whose life is falling apart. God desires that you have a flourishing marriage. Therefore, it is important to align yourself with individuals who lead lives of integrity. Such individuals will have your best interest at heart. They, in turn, will challenge you to live a life of integrity.

Developing Self-Control

It goes without saying that self-discipline is a key component to having a thriving marriage. Having godly leaders or role models also helps with developing self-control. There are many areas in life where self-control is required, such as one's temper, eating habits, sexual appetites, spending habits, hobbies, leisure activities, and drinking, to name a few. However, for all intents and purposes, our main focus in this section deals primarily with sexual appetites. It is one of the areas in marriage that couples often overlook at first yet, if left unchecked, can be destructive. Proverbs 25:28 says, "A person without self-control is like a city with broken-down walls." There is not much dissertation that is needed for this particular verse. It speaks clearly for itself. More often than usual, couples discover, throughout the course of their marriage, that there are self-control gaps that were not caught at the beginning stages of the relationship. It is human nature, due to guilt and shame, to hide our inner demons. Sooner or later though, the truth always comes to the surface. In this book, couples are encouraged to expose inner demons or secret sins and struggles to avoid the pitfalls that are inevitable as a result. *Whatever you expose cannot and will not expose you.* The reverse of this is also true. Individuals enter the marriage thinking, *I can deal with this thing all on my own, and eventually I will beat it.* While that can be true sometimes, it seldom is. The reality is that you will keep digging yourself further and further into a thing if you do not get help. Here are some pitfalls/habits that demonstrate a lack of self-control:

- ❖ Pornography
- ❖ Masturbation
- ❖ Perverted sexual fantasies
- ❖ Keeping close friends of the opposite sex
- ❖ Online social media chat rooms with the opposite sex
- ❖ Keeping in touch with exes
- ❖ Emotional affairs

Under no circumstances are any of the habits listed above acceptable. While some may feel that it's harmless to participate in pornography, masturbation, etc., they open doors to other dangers. Both husband and wife must be in agreement where this is concerned. Consequently, one of the dangers in having these open doors is that it creates false expectations of yourself and your spouse. These are expectations that shouldn't be there in the first place. For instance, someone with perverted sexual fantasies will have expectations of their partner that may fall flat. The other spouse may not be willing to deliver on these twisted fantasies. As a result, this could cause rifts that potentially will compound over time. In addition, you can complicate matters even more, for instance, if we add "keeping in touch with an ex" into the mix. In this scenario, you run the danger of sparking an old flame, which, of course, will be very dangerous to your marriage. Understandably, in some circumstances, it is unavoidable, when there is a child or children involved from a previous relationship, to completely sever all ties with an ex. It is the exception, not the norm. Any type of interaction that is shared with the opposite sex should always remain strictly platonic, avoiding room for emotional ties to form. This is a good safeguard or principle to live by.

Developing self-control guards the integrity of the marital relationship and causes its foundation to be rooted in truth. If truth is found at the foundation of your marriage, it leaves no room for facade. One lie leads to another. It eventually snowballs into a destructive force. On the flip side, here are some good habits that cultivate self-control in your marriage:

- ✓ Setting boundaries in the things you view (i.e., magazines, movies, and internet)
- ✓ Eliminating close bonds with the opposite sex (i.e., coworkers, exes, etc.)
- ✓ Being accountable to each other
- ✓ Being honest with yourself
- ✓ Being willing to expose bad habits
- ✓ Not entertaining wrong thoughts
- ✓ Reading and meditating on God's Word daily
- ✓ Cultivating a repented heart before God and your spouse

If you are choosing to live a disciplined life, you must have healthy desires that are in line with God's Word.

Self-discipline/control does not come overnight. It takes work on a daily basis. It is clear by account of scripture in Genesis 3:6, where it tells us, "When the woman Eve *saw* that the *fruit* of the *tree* was *good* for food and pleasing to the eye and also desirable for *gaining wisdom*, she took some and *ate* it. She also gave some to her husband who was with her, and he ate it" (emphasis added). Notice the progression that took place in the Garden of Eden. First, she saw the fruit on the tree, then she justified that it was good, she began to fantasize about the benefits of her action, and then she ate it. Not only did she eat of the fruit, but she also involved her husband, and he ate.

The Cycle of Desire

Saw—refers to the eyes
Fruit—represents the thing you desire
Tree—represents rooted behaviors
Good—represents justifying the behavior
Gaining wisdom—represents flirting with wrong desires or fantasies
Ate—represents giving in to the desire

Like Eve, many of us have desires that, at first, may seem harmless but, in the end, prove destructive. Oftentimes, when you surround yourself with others who have wrong thinking, behaviors, and desires, eventually that rubs off. Adam is that example. Though Adam loved Eve, he consented to participate in an act that resulted in them defiling the natural order of what God originally intended for them. Even though this story is from an ancient text, it is yet still relevant to our lives today. There's an old saying that says, "Not all that glitters is gold." Sometimes the things we desire aren't always good for us. Yet if we are to be truthful to ourselves, we desire them anyway. If we aren't careful at times, we will even begin to desire that which belongs to someone else. Desires and self-control work parallel. Good desires create good self-discipline and vice versa. If your desires aren't kept in check, they will begin to make demands. Whatever you desire is what you will go searching for. Take window-shopping for instance. When looking at something appealing in the store display, as you stroll through the mall, it may catch your eye at first glance. You look over again, and you begin to admire the ensemble. You then walk closer toward it and take a better look. You now begin to picture yourself wearing the apparel or having it in your home or using it (whether it is clothing, furniture, electronics, or a car). If you don't walk away, it is more than likely that you will walk into the store and buy it. While some people are more impulsive than others, when it comes to shopping, both types of people are subject to temptation. The danger lies in the incubation period of a thought. While you may not be able to control your field of vision, you can gauge your actions. The same is true when sexual desires present themselves. In the book of Psalm 37:4, it says, "Delight yourself also in the Lord, and He shall give you the desires of your heart." It is important that our desires for godly things are what he desires for us. It is a fact that wrong desires attract friends with the same desires. As it relates to your marriage, it is a good practice to be around friends or other couples with godly desires. Watch the conversations you entertain. It could be at work, it could be at church, or it could be in the home. It is important to establish boundaries for your ear gates, your eye gates, and your mouth gates. If you think there is nothing in life that can't take you out, wrong desires sure can.

Wrong desires can also be a result of soul ties from past relationships. A soul tie is a spiritual/emotional bond you have to someone after being intimate with them. This usually occurs after a sexual encounter with another person. It is a very tight bond that is difficult to break. This is because two souls have been knitted together and have become one flesh. When this happens, even long after that relationship has been severed, the desire to relive a nostalgic moment may still linger. This is why married couples should be sure to rid themselves of soul ties before entering the marriage relationship. If not, you will never be satisfied. Soul ties can cause you to compare your spouse to a past sexual partner. This type of behavior is not only unhealthy, but it is also unfair as it infringes on your spouse's ability to satisfy your desires. It is important as married couples that we keep our sexual desires in check. It is noteworthy to mention that while being married affords you the privilege of being intimate and expressive with your spouse, there are parameters that must be in place. These parameters must fall in line with God's intent for the wholesomeness of the relationship as it relates to sexual practices. Therefore, the Word of God sets the standard, not society. The fruits of self-control, coupled with good desires, are

✓ a structured lifestyle,
✓ you developing good habits,
✓ sustaining and strengthening moral values,
✓ you gaining wisdom,
✓ you reaping family blessings due to your obedience,
✓ your blind spots being kept in check.

Assignment

Think of areas in your life where you have wrong desires and where you are lacking self-control. Write how the principles outlined have helped you recognize areas in your relationship that need to be submitted in prayer to God.

_____

_____

_____

_____

_____

_____

The Age of Social Media

In the last few decades, the explosion of social media has propelled the behavioral changes in society to an exponential degree. We are being governed by a "politically correct" system that dictates the human interaction, such as our values, our beliefs, our self-image, and our psyche. Social media isn't all bad. There are good aspects to social media that serve as tools to make us productive individuals. On the flip side, however, because we are so interconnected, the ideas, thoughts, concepts, and behaviors that are propagated throughout diverse media outlets begin to amalgamate in the human mind. We are so strongly influenced collectively by what we see and hear and what is popularly discussed among our peers and those we associate with. What is portrayed in the media shapes our culture as we know it. We begin to think alike because we have been conditioned to do so. As a result, what we see and hear becomes the status quo. We've allowed ourselves to become mindless zombies who let others tell us what to think and how to live. We no longer think for ourselves. We have become slaves to the world of algorithms.

As you are reading this, you might be asking yourself, "How is this related to marriage?" We have allowed social media to redefine our worldview in terms of our values, beliefs, culture, and relationships. While our worldviews can change, our only authority being the Bible and its principles never changes. As Christians, it is imperative that we gauge our lives according to God's Word, not social media or any other source for that matter. Despite the barriers of time, culture, language, race, and scientific achievements, the Bible is still relevant and stands the test of truth. Its principles are solid and infallible. Social media today portrays a much-distorted view of what marriage should look like.

What Social Media Says	**What the Bible Says**
— Promiscuity and perversion are acceptable.	— Remain pure.
— Love is conditional.	— Love never fails.
— Abortion is glorified.	— Thou shall not murder.
— Be independent.	— Be interdependent (a body).
— Same-sex marriage is an option.	— One man with one woman.
— Covetousness is a good motivator (the Jones's effect).	— Work diligently and do not covet your neighbor's.
— Children are their own authority.	— Children, obey your parents (authority).

Social media is a powerful thing, and if we're not careful, we will begin to shape our lives around all it promotes. We have to be careful not to allow ourselves to be dictated by it. An example of this could be dating sites. They allow you to customize your ideal man or woman. They create this false expectation that if your ideal partner has your specified qualities, then the relationship is more likely to work. While in some cases this may be true, it's the exception, not the rule. A marriage works based on both individuals' willingness for it to do so. It doesn't matter if you have found the ideal "match" according to the dating site of your choice, what truly validates a relationship is your choice to love someone unconditionally. No strings attached. Some of the dangers are that people can falsify their characters on their profiles. Also, the idea in your head may not be God's idea of who is best for you. In fact, he may have the exact opposite type of person for you in mind, the kind you always said you'd "never" be with. Often when you say *never*, that's exactly what you end up with.

Another danger of social media is simply our ability to reconnect with past "crushes." While this act may seem completely innocent and harmless, it is deceiving. Perhaps you may have known this person from childhood or high school and, in your mind, the emotions you once shared were left in the past. This may not be true for both parties. The risk in this scenario is the possibility of evoking old memories that could reignite old feelings that may have never been expressed. As good intentioned as one may be as one types behind the comfort of one's computer screen, danger lurks behind every word that is exchanged. The internet makes it very easy to be too comfortable and open when you are interacting with such an individual. In an online article called "Is Social Networking Destroying Marriages? 5 Tips to Protect Your Partnership" written on March 20 2012, by Tina Ray, she wrote that divorce attorneys regularly search Facebook for evidence of infidelity, spending money, and assets. In fact, in a recent American Academy of Matrimonial Lawyers study, 66 percent of divorce attorneys surveyed said Facebook was their primary online resource for case evidence. About 81 percent "have seen an increase in the number of cases using social networking evidence during the past five years." The article continued to say that Steven Kimmons, PhD, of Loyola University Medical Center in Maywood, Illinois, describes one way such extramarital relationships start. "One spouse connects online with someone they knew from high school. The person is emotionally available, and they start communicating through Facebook," Kimmons explains. "Within a short amount of time, the sharing of personal stories can lead to a deepened sense of intimacy, which, in turn, can point the couple in the direction of physical contact." An errant spouse may not set out to do wrong. The person may simply be curious about what an old friend or an old flame is doing and decides to say hello online, Kimmons says. If the errant spouse ends up talking to the old friend more often than their own spouse, he says, "You don't need a fancy psychological study to conclude that I'm more likely to fall in love with the person I talk to five times a week because I have more contact with that person." The beginning of such a relationship may be innocent, but its continuation is not.

There are websites that are specifically devoted to luring married men and women into cyberaffairs. Unfortunately, these websites are getting more and more popular every day and are frequent pop-ups on social media. The bombardment of these sites is inevitable yet avoidable. In a recent scandal surrounding the Ashley Madison dating site catering to extramarital affairs, upon their profiles being publicly exposed, many of its members have even committed suicide due to the unbearable shame. This may be an extreme example, but not a far-fetched one.

The scripture tells us in Proverbs 14:12, "There is a path before each person that seems right, but it ends in death." It is very important that we guard our marriages from the pit of social media. Social media acts as a gateway for illicit behaviors that could destroy our marriages.

Movies and music are two of the most powerful influences of the twenty-first century. The lyrical contents and the explicit messages therein play a huge role in the way couples interact in marital relationships. The Hollywood box office hit *50 Shades of Grey* should by no means be considered an exemplary guide to what a healthy and godly relationship should look like. There's nothing gray about it; it's actually *black*. Hollywood spends billions of dollars each year conditioning our minds to believe that such acts are acceptable in all forms of intimate relationships. This movie, among others, promotes violence and abuse as viable behaviors in a relationship. Trying to live out these erotic, violent, sexual fantasies preconditions the mind to accept that these dangerous behaviors are normal. Why are these behaviors not OK within the parameters of marriage? Because these are perverted behaviors that mimic all the qualities of Satan. He is domineering, violent, masochistic, sadistic, and emotionally and psychologically destructive. These behaviors dishonor God and his design for the marriage dynamic. Not to mention these are the very same twisted acts that are performed in satanic occult rituals. Music, on the other hand, offers no subtlety in its approach either. Mainstream artists promote selfish, vulgar, violent, no-strings-attached, temporary relationships. They cheapen the intended sacredness of sex and promote instant gratification and only short-term commitments, if any at all. It is said that music is one of the only things in life that engage 100 percent of our brains. With that fact, it influences us in more ways than we can imagine. Social media allows music and movies to go viral and be accessible to the masses. Marshall McLuhan coined the phrase "The medium is the message." If we aren't careful as married couples, we can become victims to the messages that are being propagated through these outlets.

Chapter 5

The Mission and Vision for Your Marriage

Previously we talked about marriage as a covenant, but in light of all that, marriage takes hard work. Don't be alarmed by the word *hard*. Anything that is worth doing takes sacrifice, and sacrifice takes hard work. There are many sacrifices that a couple may have to take throughout the lifetime of their marriage. When it's all said and done, most couples will admit it was worth every moment. A marriage that works takes work. Hard work takes planning, and planning takes having a mission and vision in mind. Harvey MacKay once said, "When you fail to plan, you plan to fail."

People often confuse a mission statement with a vision statement. While they are similar and they go hand in hand, they are not the same. A mission statement is a short-term goal for the present, as opposed to a vision statement, which is a long-term goal forecasting future plans. You can't have one without the other. Having a mission for your marriage is likened to a stepping-stone toward one's desired destination.

Your marriage should not be treated like a business, but in essence, it has some characteristics of what a business venture looks like. If you've ever run a small business, you'd see the parallel in this scenario. Let's say you have a vision to own a five-star family restaurant. You know that the odds are stacked up against you, because statistically 50 percent of restaurants fail within the first three to five years. One of the major reasons for this is that most small-business owners aren't in it for the long haul, only for the short-term gain. It is your mission statement that causes you to build an unshakeable, solid foundation for your vision. Whatever or however you choose to invest in the short term will determine your ability to endure in your future. Your mission creates a rock-solid foundation that is built to last.

Subsequently, society today has also reduced marriage to a three- to five-year life span. There is not much faith in marriage as we know it. Most couples enter the marriage relationship with the fear that they may not make it over the five-year hump. They dread the thought that they may become a statistic as many have. It is vitally important that marriage couples have a vision and a mission that is sustainable. Couples must also have a mission and a vision that is flexible. This will prepare them for possible changes that may occur along the way. Having a flexible mission and vision will save couples the heartbreak of unexpected issues that life may throw at them—for instance, the news of an unplanned pregnancy, the death of a loved one, the need to move suddenly for whatever the reason, etc. If your mission or vision is flexible, the thought of making minor adjustments when necessary may not be as traumatic. As the saying goes, "Life happens," and indeed it does. In fact, there are times when you may have to scrap your vision and mission altogether. Your vision should include a sense of adventure. It will come in handy, especially for those times when "life happens" and things don't turn out as planned. Sometimes, even when you have a vision in place, the most unexpected happens. Don't allow that to dishevel you. Instead, allow those obstacles to become building blocks to strengthen your team skills as a couple. You can make many plans, but the Lord's purpose will prevail (Proverbs 19:21). There may come a time when you draw up a great vision together and it seems to make perfect sense, so much so that you can't imagine any other vision but that one. Just when you think you have it down pat, something crazy happens and your entire plan falls to shambles. It's so easy to get disgruntled and discouraged. Don't allow this to tear your marriage apart. Don't see this as an obstacle; instead, see this as an opportunity to allow God to guide you to the next stepping-stone in your life's journey. God has a way of totally closing a door in your face so fast you won't know what hit you, only to open a bigger door to your destiny. He also does this to test your faith as a couple and your patience. Will you trust God when your source of security falls flat? Will you trust him when the rug is pulled out from beneath you? Perhaps in your plan you did everything right and followed every strategy to a tee to realize your vision, and yet your plans got completely derailed. While this may seem like a reality at the time, you should instead take this as an opportunity to partner with God and his vision for your life. Ultimately, he will surprise you if you surrender your goals, dreams, and vision. Even if you are feeling that you've hit rock bottom, you need to trust God through the process—because sometimes God will allow what you've built to be broken-down in order to rebuild it with the right foundation. This process hurts, but it is necessary and beneficial to your relationship with God and your spouse. It will build perseverance, endurance, character, patience, trust, unity, and rock-solid, unwavering faith. Your vision and your mission, no matter how well planned out they may be, will encounter storms.

Why do couples need a mission and a vision for their marriage?

✓ It keeps them focused on their goals.
✓ It prepares them for unexpected bumps ahead.
✓ It keeps them disciplined.
✓ It exposes their blind spots.
✓ It creates momentum to achieve.
✓ It creates strategies.
✓ It creates clarity.
✓ It gives purpose and long-term benefits.
✓ It creates perseverance.

Whenever you achieve your goals, however simple they may seem, celebrate those achievements. When you celebrate your achievements, you both are motivated to tackle the next one in line. Whether it is the purchase of your first home together or a financial achievement, it is a healthy practice to slow down and celebrate your achievements along the way. It is OK to live in the moment. Being ambitious is a good thing when used as a kick start to be driven toward your goals. However, it can also be dangerous if you indulge in it and become so consumed that you miss the little moments that make up the puzzle pieces of your life. Celebrate the milestones. Ecclesiastes 8:15 says, "So I recommend having fun, because there is nothing better for people in this world than to eat, drink, and enjoy life. That way they will experience some happiness along with all the hard work God gives them under the sun." This approach will even extend your life span. Eliminate anxiety about future events and plans now that you have surrendered them to God. For added confirmation, Matthew 6:27 clearly tells us, "And which of you by being anxious can add a single hour to his span of life?"

Your Marriage Is a Ministry

You have got to see your marriage as a ministry. It's not just any ministry; it is your first ministry. It is about couples serving each other, and as they do so, they also learn to serve others. It is imperative that the home front is first and foremost as it relates to your service to the Lord. In 1 Timothy 5:8, it says, "Anyone who does not provide for their relatives, and especially for their own household, has denied the faith and is worse than an unbeliever." It is OK to be zealous in the faith, but do not get wrapped up in false humility. Be careful of the dangers of overzealousness. One can get so caught up in one's zeal and emotional ties to a particular ministry that one neglects the most important one of all: the home front. Don't feel guilty or pressured to be a part of everything. It is important to learn what it means to prioritize one's family life. After all, God is a god not of disorder but of peace. The family is a reflection of the character of God. Father, Son, and Holy Spirit do not contradict. They work harmoniously. Do not allow your ambitions to drive a wedge between you and your family. There needs to be clear boundaries and a balance between your outside ministry and your family ministry. Be sure to recognize the things that put strain on your marriage. For some, the variables are completely different. For instance, for one couple, traveling apart for extended periods of time for ministry may work. For another couple, it may not. It may put a strain on the relationship. How do you know when it is right and when it is not? If the distance creates a strain, couples need to reevaluate if continued traveling is appropriate. Do not be afraid to surrender your own ambitions in exchange for God's ultimate plan and purpose for your life. Perhaps, this may mean stepping back and laying down the thing you have always dreamed of doing and allowing God to refine his perfect will for your family. Don't have the mentality of "Before I met my spouse, I was doing this thing, so why should I lay it down at this time?" We should bear in mind that, ultimately, God's will is what prevails in the end. Laying down your plans is not giving up your dreams, but it's an act of surrender and humility as you are placing them in his hands. Inevitably, God will always perfect that which he has started in your life. The beauty about God is that when you surrender something to him, he gives you something even better in return. Who are we to instruct God on the desired path we must take to our destiny? The idea here is trusting that God is in total control and has your best interest at heart.

> *For I know the plans I have for you,*
> *plans to prosper you*
> *and give you a hope and a future.*
> *(Jeremiah 29:11)*

You and your spouse are two vast human beings. God uniquely designed you as such. For the most part, as human beings, we all have a particular path that we desire to take throughout our lifetime. As a result, we define ourselves by the things we do, rather than who he truly designed us to be. For example, you are an artist, and that's how others see you, and as a result, that is how you define yourself. In fact, there's more to you than just being an artist or a lawyer or a doctor or even a factory worker. While it is important to have a balanced perspective of one's self, the true you is wrapped up inside. One of the roles of a spouse is to pull out the best of the other and nurture it together as you pursue God's purpose for your lives.

Always remember, God can use you right where you are, be it in your home, to be an encouragement to a loved one or in your community. Not everyone is called to a "pulpit ministry." Your ministry goes as far as the sphere of your influence reaches. In fact, your ministry is in your hands, your feet, and your mouth. It is where you go, what you say, and whom you touch. If we have this balanced view of what ministry is or the possibility of what ministry could bring, then we won't become frustrated at where we are right now. Perhaps you may think you should be further in life when, in actuality, the process and the journey that refine you are just as important as your destination. In fact, they build character, which is what will sustain you in the ministry that God has planned for your lives together. It is important to maintain a realistic perspective of where you are.

This ministry that God has given you both is an assignment. This assignment requires an enormous amount of teamwork. The scriptures were given to us to guide us and build us up, to correct us, and to inspire us. However, they should not be used for coercion or manipulation and to assert authority one over the other. In contrast to these, rather we should learn what it means to increase and decrease at the appropriate moments. For instance, the wife is a pastor, and the husband is an elder in the church. They both have a voice in this scenario; however, being that the wife is the pastor, her husband would be under her authority. But outside the roles they play in church, the wife would now be under the authority of her husband as he is the head of the home. Do not misunderstand the word *authority* here as it is referring to merely roles as opposed to subordinates.

In this next scenario, Richard and Jane are out for dinner with Daniel and Samantha. At some point during conversation, Daniel and Samantha open up about a delicate situation they are going through. Jane can relate to this and offers a word of advice and comfort. Richard is sensitive to what Jane has to offer at this time and quietly and sympathetically listens until Jane has fully voiced her thoughts to the couple. At this point, his kind, attentive gestures such as a nod of affirmation are sufficient.

A negative example of this would be Richard and Jane both jumping into the conversation at the same time. Neither of them is willing to let the other speak. One person speaks, and the other cuts in, not allowing the other to finish their statement. It is evident that Richard and Jane are trying to outtalk or outsmart each other as they debate. What should have been a constructive conversation between two couples ended up being a competition between two people while the other couple remains dumbfounded. Neither of them is willing to give in or submit to the other's point of view. We should never have an attitude of competition.

When you are married, you are on the same team. This means that by bringing out the best in each other, when one is at one's stronger point, it is okay to decrease and let them increase and vice versa. This creates a sense of interdependency and unity. It also creates a dynamic that is visible to others who are looking for a godly marriage they can look up to. Your marriage should not be about just going through the motions. People are looking for real examples from real people who go through real stuff. Your marriage assignment will be tried and tested. You will experience private cries and pains, but God will use all that to establish his plans in your lives. Honor each other as you honor the Lord in this ministry called marriage. Honor and respect are some of the pillars of a marriage—when you honor your spouse, you are honouring God.

Building on a Rock-Solid Foundation

> *Anyone who listens to my teaching and follows it is wise, like a person who builds a house on solid rock. Though the rain comes in torrents and the floodwaters rise and the winds beat against that house, it won't collapse because it is built on bedrock. But anyone who hears my teaching and doesn't obey it is foolish, like a person who builds a house on sand. When the rains and floods come and the winds beat against that house, it will collapse with a mighty crash. (Matthew 7:24–27)*

The foundation on which you build is essential for your future together as a married couple. What foundation are you built on? Is it rock-solid? Would you say that the bedrock of your life together is built on the principles of God's Word? In the key scripture above, Jesus spoke of two kinds of individuals—the wise and the foolish. As harsh as these words may sound to most, they are the epitome of truth. In actually, the truth is often bluntly spoken and is final. In this case, Jesus spoke about what it means to build your life on a solid rock. Metaphorically, he was admonishing his audience to live their lives based on his teachings and also to model how he lived. He went on to say that those who follow his teachings are considered wise. On the flip side, those who ignore his teachings are considered foolish because their lives are built on sand, which represents their own ideology and falls short of God's wisdom. The one who builds on the rock is sure to stand, but the one who builds on the sand will collapse. You may ask, how does this relate to the marriage relationship? There are foundational principles that a godly marriage is built upon. This verse exemplifies what a strong, secure marriage should look like. It offers an anchor, which is Christ, to life's challenging moments. In a disposable-thinking culture where both Christians and non-Christians are faced with daily marital issues, this verse allows you to think like an architect. The integrity of your structure needs to be solid for the long term. No architect builds with the hopes of a structure falling apart in a couple of months or even a couple of years—it's nonsensical. Practically speaking, you would never hire such an architect. Granted, there will be circumstances in your marriage that may be challenging. They may even challenge your faith and all that you have known to be true. But the building of your foundation will require effort from both you and your spouse. If, for instance, one spouse is building and the other is tearing apart, say, the bricks of trust or of communication, the structure of the marriage will crumble. Contrary to secular beliefs, marriages still have the ability to last in a disposable-thinking culture or the status quo. The Word of God is filled with principles and tools that will sustain the life of your marriage. You just need to read it! You must be intentional and pragmatic when building your bedrock foundation.

It cannot be approached with a haphazard mentality. Both you and your spouse must have a united front when building. For example, if you both come from different cultural backgrounds, there must be a middle ground of understanding when building. While you may both have different views on social issues and family traditions, it is possible to find a balance between the two. The key is building *together.*

The foundational principles that are found in the Bible are foolproof. Those who live by these principles experience rock-solid relationships. They are able to pass down what they've learned to future generations. These are examples of building blocks that make up the foundation of a rock-solid, godly marriage relationship:

- ✓ Prayer
- ✓ Faith/trust
- ✓ Focus
- ✓ Commitment
- ✓ Humility/pliability
- ✓ Wisdom

Prayer

Without prayer, there is no true connection to God, the Father. Prayer is an active and intentional act of communication with God. Prayer should not become a chore-like activity. Couples should make an effort to pray together as much as possible. It not only strengthens their bond together but increases their intimacy with God. When two people are in agreement on any matter, they can accomplish just about anything. This same principle can be applied to prayer.

> *And again I say to you if two of you agree on earth about anything they ask it will be done for them by my Father in heaven. (Matthew 18:19)*

Faith/Trust

Having total faith in God means surrendering your own will and desires to him. When your will and desires are submitted, you can rest assured that God has your best interest at heart. This act removes all fear, worry, anxiety, insecurities, and independence. It is important that couples get to this place in their marriage with the assurance that God is in total control. All they have to do is live in the obedience of his Word. When you know that God is in control, it is a good place to start.

> *Trust in the Lord with all your heart and lean not on your own understanding; in all of your ways submit to Him, and he will make your paths straight. (Proverbs 3:5–6)*

Focus

Never lose focus of the things that are truly important—for example, God, family, ministry, financial goals, and personal development, to name a few. It is very easy to become distracted in such a fast-paced, busy day in age. Having a balanced focus is key, as well as being able to prioritize what you focus on. Distractions delay a process or your ability to accomplish your goals.

> *Let your eyes look directly ahead and let your gaze be fixed straight in front of you. (Proverbs 4:25)*

Commitment

Both you and your spouse must be committed to accomplishing your goals together, as well as reaffirming your commitment to each other. Commitment takes focus, and focus takes commitment. This goes without saying. When you are committed, you need to be 100/100, not fifty-fifty. Commitment brings forth momentum, which requires encouragement in order to thrive.

But Ruth said, "Do not urge me to leave you or to return from following you. For where you go I will go, and where you lodge I will lodge. Your people will be my people, and your God my God. Where you die I will die, and there will I be buried. May the Lord do so to me and more also if anything but death parts me from you." (Ruth 1:16–17)

Humility/Pliability

God desires for each of us to live a life of humility. Humbling yourself uplifts the other person, which brings out the best in them. When done mutually and intentionally, it brings out the best in each other. Humility allows for pliability, which opens the door for growth in your marriage. Pride can allow us to feel as though we have attained, while humility acknowledges room to learn new things.

Always be humble and gentle. Be patient which each other, making allowance for each other's faults because of your love. (Ephesians 4:2)

When pride comes, then comes disgrace, but with humility comes wisdom. (Proverbs 11:2)

Wisdom

Let wisdom be your guide as you journey together in your marriage. True wisdom comes from God; therefore, every decision that you make requires godly wisdom. You will encounter situations in life that may seem confusing—godly wisdom causes you to discern which way to go, what to say, how, and when.

If anyone lacks wisdom, you should ask God, who gives generously to all without finding fault and it will be given you. (James 1:5)

*How much better to get wisdom than gold, to
get insight rather than silver. (Proverbs 16:16)*

Money and Debt Management

It cannot be stressed enough how important it is for couples to have a united front in their marriage, especially when it comes to finances. Prior to marriage, both individuals had very different ideas about finances. One of the challenges that come with two people becoming one unit is the merging of their finances. It is important for a couple, before even entering a marriage, to understand that they need a team mentality when it comes to saving, budgeting, investing, and setting short- and long-term goals. People become funny when money is in the mix. It's like hitting a nerve. Ouch! The true character of your heart is revealed when your finances are challenged.

According to Matthew 6:21, *"For where your treasure is, there will your heart be also."*

The context of this verse is referring specifically to the treasure of your money and possessions. Money and possessions are very personal to us because, naturally, we work hard for what we earn. As a result, we become very attached to them. It's easy to get to a place of "What's mine is mine, and what's yours is yours." Not so in a marriage. Just like it is true that your marital bed is not divided, neither should your finances be. When your finances are merged, it challenges you to become accountable to each other and think like a team. Also, it creates discipline, maturity, selflessness, and unity. It's not easy, but in the long run, it is worth it. It's no big surprise that one of the most common causes of marriage breakdown is money. This should motivate us to focus and work harder and intentionally on this area. Even if it takes getting some professional insight or help in this department, it is well worth it. Hiring a financial adviser or accountant, for instance, could be the best investment you'll ever make for the sake of your marriage. In fact, our money is not actually our money after all. Everything belongs to God.

Psalm 24:1 confirms this: *"The earth is the LORD's, and everything in it, the world, and all who live in it."*

When we have this mind-set, we become more cognizant of how we use and/or steward our possessions. In order to properly manage your finances responsibly as a couple, it is wise to maintain a budget and be mindful of your debt load. Budgeting is hard and annoying at first, but it's worth it! It is like your financial GPS. Without it, you may think you know where you are going, yet you will make some wrong financial decisions that may cost you later on. If you don't have a budget, you need one. It will expose all your blind spots and bad habits. Do you often wonder where your money is going and why you are constantly broke before the month ends? Start a budget now and you will see. Why should God bless you with more if you aren't managing the little you have now? Certainly, the lottery isn't your only hope for financial freedom? Nor is budgeting by any means, but it sure positions you for a better future for you and your children. Stop buying things you don't need. Wants and needs are clearly two different things. Go on a diet if need be. Budgeting is not easy, but it sure is necessary and, more importantly, worth it. It's not too late. Start now.

Larry Sibeling says, *"Personal finance is more personal than it is finance. It's 20% head knowledge, and 80% behaviour."*

Below are some practical ways to managing your finances and maintaining a budget:

- ✓ Manage your debt load, create a budget, and live within it.
- ✓ Don't spend based on possible future events (i.e., income tax return, work bonuses, promised gifts, etc.).
- ✓ Don't create unnecessary debts.
- ✓ Limit the number of credit cards to one per household and live within a set limit.
- ✓ More cash, less credit.
- ✓ Prioritize needs vs. wants.
- ✓ Stay clear of "Buy now, pay later" schemes.
- ✓ Spend your money God's way.
- ✓ Talk about your finances and make decisions together.
- ✓ Keep each other accountable.
- ✓ Set realistic goals and review them periodically.

- ✓ Make wise investments—retirement funds, child education funds, etc.
- ✓ Tithe always and be generous in your giving.
- ✓ Trust God in the tough times—trust in something bigger than money.
- ✓ Don't risk more than you can afford to lose.
- ✓ If you lose, prepare to lose together—avoid the blame game.
- ✓ Consciously decide to abandon old mind-sets.
- ✓ Your true identity is not found in things but rather in Christ.
- ✓ Greed and speed are partners in crime—work diligently on your goals without rushing.
- ✓ Get-rich-quick pyramid schemes are not the answer.
- ✓ Include savings in your budget and stick to your commitments.
- ✓ Work toward paying of debts.

These are practical financial tools that could strengthen your marriage empire. As you can imagine, it can be extremely difficult to be part of a team that is simply not working in sync. Much like a sports team, they all anticipate the moves of their teammates. They are interdependent as they work toward a common goal. Your marriage takes teamwork. Be the best team you could possibly be. When it comes to your finances, this area of your life is a true reflection of other areas in your marriage. Guard this area of your marriage as you build together a household that is honoring the Lord. Your marriage should always strive to reflect the triune nature of God—unity is your friend.

Assignment:

In what ways are you building your relationship on a "rock solid" foundation? In what areas can you improve?

Can you identify tools that will make you better steward your finances?

_____

_____

Chapter 6

Knowing Your Roles in the Marriage

Gender roles are often misconceived in today's culture. In fact, our past traditions have a lot to do with how we perceive these roles as well. People have misconstrued the biblical interpretation of what God intended. There are three extreme perceptions that have all missed the mark. These views are as follows:

The Old-Fashioned/Traditional View

In this perception, the male is seen as a domineering figure, while the woman is considered less significant—the master-servant relationship.

The Feminist View

Then there is the feminist movement, where the roles are completely reversed. This particular movement began in the early 1960s and 1970s in an attempt to equalize women's rights with men's. Basically, the feminist agenda started off as a fight for equal pay and to allow women to make decisions without the approval of men or husbands.

Postmodern View

Third and most popular, there is the postmodern mind-set. This view has been around since the 1900s and was popularized by the atheist philosopher Friedrich Nietzsche. Postmodernism says there is no objective or absolute truth. It is therefore relatively left up to individuals, cultures, and communities to interpret what truth is.

As it pertains to gender roles, they are completely interchangeable without gender distinction. In fact, there is a stigma attached to gender-role association. The roles must be interchangeable in order to render them equal. *Equality* has become a very popular terminology in our present world to even the playing field by eliminating specific gender (male/female) identity. None of these ideas support the biblical view. They vehemently oppose it, in fact.

It is important that we combat and reject what is considered "politically correct" in order to remain grounded in the biblical context. Why would God create roles if they are of no importance according to the standards of our society? In this section, we will examine the male and female roles as laid out in scripture:

A Husband's Roles: Leader (Primary), Lover, Provider, Priest, Protector

★Leader

Men are called as role models for their wives as well as their children. The Lord God has placed men in a headship position. They are to lead not just by word but, most importantly, by example. In today's feminist-driven culture, the need for strong male leadership roles on the home front is further reinforced. Men need not shy away from their God-given responsibilities. In order to lead the home effectively, one must also be a leader of himself, which requires integrity and character that portrays the heart of God. In the role of leader, the man is not a slave master. One of his main attributes is love.

Ephesians 5:22–23

> Wives, submit yourselves unto your own husbands, as unto the Lord. For the husband is the **head** of the wife, even as Christ is the head of the church: and he is the saviour of the body.

*Lover

The apostle Paul drew a very distinctive parallel between Christ and his church and between the husband and the wife. This love is sacrificial in nature. It is with that same sacrificial approach that men ought to love their wives. This love encompasses all three types of love described in the Bible: agape (divine love), philos (friendly/family love), and eros (romantic love). These three pillars of love make up the true dynamic of what a godly marriage is based upon. It is important to keep in mind that if any of these pillars are lacking, you can be sure that the marriage will suffer.

Ephesians 5:25–28

> Husbands, **love** your wives, even as Christ also **loved** the church, and gave himself for it; That he might sanctify and cleanse it with the washing of water by the word, That he might present it to himself a glorious church, not having spot, or wrinkle, or any such thing; but that it should be holy and without blemish. So ought men to **love** their wives as their own bodies. He that **loveth** his wife loveth himself.

*Provider

Traditionally, men are known as hunter-gatherers. They are considered the breadwinners of the family. Though this tradition has changed in the modern era, it does not diminish the man's role. In a society in which the gender roles have become blurred, it is noteworthy to remember that God's Word trumps cultural norms. Biblically speaking, the man's role is to provide for his family. When we stray from God's design, something will inevitably fall out of balance in the family dynamic. Somewhere along the line, pressure will mount despite your best efforts. Having said that, there are circumstances in which roles such as this one may be interchanged. For instance, in the case of a disability, the wife may be required to step up to the plate as the main provider. This does not, however, negate the man's primary role as leader.

1 Timothy 5:8

> But if any **provide** not for his own, and specially for those of his own house, he hath denied the faith, and is worse than an infidel.

*Priest

The man sets the spiritual temperature in the home. He is the mediator for his family to God, just as Jesus mediates on behalf of the church (his bride) to God, the Father. In this role, the man leads by example and challenges his family to foster a deeper relationship with God. In many cases, men don't see themselves as priests; as a result, the spiritual dynamic of the family falls short. The role of priest is not a pastoral one in the sense of a church leader but, rather, the spiritual head of the family. He spends time in prayer for the needs and concerns of his family, just as Jesus mediates on our behalf to the Father.

1 Corinthians 11:3

> But I would have you know, that the head of every man is Christ; and the head of the woman *is* the man; and the head of Christ *is* God.

Ephesians 6:4

> And, ye fathers, provoke not your children to wrath: but bring them up in the nurture and admonition of the Lord.

*Protector

It is incumbent on the husband to provide safety and refuge for his wife and home. It is imperative to foster an environment in which his wife feels emotionally, physically, and spiritually protected. The protector takes responsibility for the welfare of his family. He seeks to provide both grace and justice for them. Security is his highest priority. He is quick to forgive, provides shelter, and administers loving discipline to the family unit. He seeks to bring honor to his household. He is a reflection of Jesus in his role of protector.

Colossians 3:19

> Husbands, love *your* wives, and be not bitter against them.

1 Peter 3:7

> Likewise, ye husbands, dwell with *them* according to knowledge, giving honour unto the wife, as unto the weaker vessel, and as being heirs together of the grace of life; that your prayers be not hindered.

A Wife's Roles: Helper (Primary), Nurturer, Counselor, Visionary, Organizer

★Helper

God's original plan for marriage, as outlined in the book of Genesis, portrays the main role of the wife as a supportive one. In her supporting role, she is seen as a complement to her husband, not a subjugated function as some often misconstrue. She is not of lesser value but rather a completion of her husband. The two together functioning in their unique roles, as designed, can be a powerful force for good. We believe that behind every great husband, there is a supportive wife.

Genesis 2:20–24

And Adam gave names to all cattle, and to the fowl of the air, and to every beast of the field; but for Adam there was not found an **help** meet for him.

The Creation of Woman

And the LORD God caused a deep sleep to fall upon Adam, and he slept: and he took one of his ribs, and closed up the flesh instead thereof; And the rib, which the LORD God had taken from man, made he a woman, and brought her unto the man. And Adam said, This *is* now bone of my bones, and flesh of my flesh: she shall be called Woman, because she was taken out of Man. Therefore shall a man leave his father and his mother, and shall cleave unto his wife: and they shall be one flesh.

★Nurturer

As the nurturer, the woman fosters an emotional, physical, and spiritual bond with her husband and household. She is industrious, laser focused, and the first responder to the needs of her family. There is a gentleness about her that resembles the healing touch of the Holy Spirit. This is an innate quality that God has so uniquely woven into the character of the woman. There is a notion, however, in today's modern society that places a stigma on this particular quality in women. Media often portrays and glamorizes women as dominant, independent, masculine-like individuals. The idea of a nurturing woman has become cliché. For some, it is only a nostalgic thought, while for many, the idea of a nurturing woman is associated with weakness, subjugation, and boredom. In a marriage relationship, the woman must be intentional about tapping into this innate gift.

Proverbs 31:12–17

She will do him good and not evil all the days of her life. She seeketh wool, and flax, and worketh willingly with her hands. She is like the merchants' ships; she bringeth her food from afar. She riseth also while it is yet night, and *giveth meat to her household*, and a portion to her maidens. She considereth a field, and buyeth it: with the fruit of her hands she planteth a vineyard. She girdeth her loins with strength, and strengtheneth her arms.

★Counselor / Voice of Wisdom / Encourager

Much like the role of the Holy Spirit (Paraclete), the woman's role is to "come alongside" and "counsel and support" her husband. She is built to discern and heed the promptings within her spirit to gently guide and offer a voice of wisdom to her husband. She uses this gift to build him up and enhance his performance in his primary role of leader. She inspires, encourages, and brings out the best in him.

Proverbs 31:26

She openeth her mouth with **wisdom**; and in her tongue *is* the law of *kindness*.

★Visionary

As a visionary, a wife has the ability to foresee and to visualize outcomes in advance. Before executing a project, she uses her incredible intuition as a guide to keep her focused in planning and decision-making. She uses this skill as a compass for future family endeavors. The visionary wife is always looking out for the best interest of her family as a unit. She can discern when to work in the background, so to speak, allowing others to shine. She does not succumb to the pressures of a self-centered culture.

Proverbs 31:18

She **perceiveth** that her merchandise *is* good: her candle goeth not out by night.

★Organizer

As an organizer, she oversees the affairs of the family. She manages and delegates tasks accordingly. She is an incredibly hardworking multitasker. She is thorough in executing her tasks. It is normal for most women to be viewed as overachievers and even super moms or super wives due to the unrealistic expectations they are burdened with by society. In this role, the wife understands that her true strength comes from the Lord and not herself. It is all too common for women to take on more than they can handle and end up burning out. Remaining open and sensitive to God's direction is the key to being the most efficient organizer you can be. Learning to say no can be one of the hardest mental struggles. Discerning quality from quantity of activities is crucial. Organizer does not equate to overachiever. It is very difficult to serve your family if you become emotionally, physically, and psychologically overwhelmed and/or drained. It is imperative to set realistic expectations for yourself and your family in order to avoid this pitfall.

Proverbs 31:27

> She *looketh well* to the ways of her house-
> hold, and eateth not the bread of idleness.

Introspective Questions before Entering a Covenant Relationship

What have you learned from past relationships, and how will it impact you now?

Are you healed from (a) previous relationship(s)?

Did you pray about the spouse God intended for you? Provide details.

What are the characteristics of your ideal spouse?

How do you know you are ready to love again?

Chapter 7

What Love Is—Verb or Noun?

In a previous chapter "What Love Is Not," we discussed precisely that. This chapter specifically deals with what love *is*. Love is the glue that holds the marriage relationship together. It is extremely multifaceted in nature. When we look at love in the Hollywood sense, it is reduced to a mere idea. It is placed under the noun category. It is a fleeting, euphoric, rebellious, temperamental, and unpredictable spell or feeling. On the contrary, God's definition of love is quite different. It is, in essence, a verb.

> Love suffers long *and* is kind; love does not envy; love does not parade itself, is not puffed up; does not behave rudely, does not seek its own, is not provoked, thinks no evil; does not rejoice in iniquity, but rejoices in the truth; bears all things, believes all things, hopes all things, endures all things. (1 Corinthians 13:4–7 NKJV)

Love is not a vague idea or feeling. It is so much more. It requires an action and a response. True love humbles us and causes us to put the other person above ourselves. It encompasses all the concepts that were discussed in this book. Let's take a moment to break down the actions of love.

1. *Love suffers long.* The true test of love requires "stick-to-it-iveness." It doesn't run at the first sign of trouble. It seeks resolutions. It is interesting that the writer starts off the

definition of love by admonishing us of the suffering that comes with love. All too often, we expect a free ride from love. If it's too hard, we don't want it. We often want all the benefits without counting the costs. Love can be beautiful and messy, all at the same time. It doesn't just offer us a buffet of good things and happiness. There are seasons of sadness, brokenness, mourning, and heartache. The scripture encourages us to anticipate and embrace these things as they come.

2. *Love is kind.* Ironically, the writer not only warns us to expect suffering but also encourages us to be kind in the process. As if the concept of suffering isn't bad enough. This is truly the moment where God's grace is needed most. True love proceeds from God, not from our own strength. It takes the burden off our shoulders and puts it on Christ's. Let's face it, without God's Spirit in us, it is almost impossible to be kind in certain day-to-day encounters—especially when we are suffering. This extends beyond the marriage relationship. It reaches into our places of employment, our communities, and our social circles.

3. *Love rejoices in the truth.* Because love, in its essence, strives for the best interest of another, it is only natural that it must be honest. The truth sets you free, while lies, even when used in the most well-intentioned of ways, say, to "protect" a loved one, never end well. The truth always prevails—whether it is expressed sooner or revealed later. It will always surface. Honesty is always the best-case scenario, even though it may hurt at first. Truth brings healing.

4. *Love bears all things.* Aren't you thankful for Jesus when you read this? Nobody enjoys carrying a burden; let's face it! But that's just selfishness speaking, right? This is another test to truly know whether you love someone. It all spurs from the sacrifice Christ made for us at the cross; that gratitude spills into our grace for others. The Holy Spirit empowers us to take on one another's burdens—

willingly! Also, love doesn't discriminate in its actions. It doesn't select which burdens to carry on any given day or period of time—it just bears. It is amazing what can come out of this practice. It has a boomerang effect. It is contagious. When we learn to carry one another's burdens, the load is lightened, and we stop looking at it as a chore. We mustn't forget—when Christ is in the center, he carries the heavy end of our burdens (Matthew 11:30).

5. *Love believes all things.* Everywhere we look, we are surrounded by lies. We have all been lied to, to some degree. Perhaps you were badly hurt by one person's lies, and you've never really recovered since. This makes it very difficult to trust again. It is in our human nature to respond in defensiveness based on past experience. Living this way toward your spouse, however, will hinder the relationship on so many levels. Intimacy is the first thing to suffer. When you lose trust, you begin to live in isolation. Unity breaks down. Communication follows. You get the picture. It is imperative that you take the risk of believing again—otherwise, you will never truly enjoy the fruits of a healthy marriage relationship. There are instances where you or your spouse may be the one to have failed miserably in this department; this still applies. There is a childlike quality to love in that it dares to believe even in the most hopeless situations. Learn to forgive and leave the past in the past. Healing is possible with Christ. It will be difficult, but completely worthwhile.

6. *Love hopes all things.* Ever heard of the old adage "Hope is the last thing you lose" or "Where there is life, there is hope"? If only we could live this! In a world of skepticism, hatred, violence, and just about any other evil, it is easy to become jaded to hope. When our focus is in the right place, however, hope is restored. When our gaze is on Christ, we are constantly reminded that we are his children and that eternal bliss awaits us after this life. That alone is an unlimited source of hope! When applied to

our daily lives, something amazing happens—we begin to see through the lens of Christ. All things are possible with God. We ought to live this way, especially in our relationships. Will you dare to hope in the most seemingly hopeless situations? God is always faithful, even when we're not, and he delights in surprising us with his goodness.

7. *Love endures all things.* Endurance refers to longevity—now there's a term that rings antiquated thoughts of this day and age! Our culture is drowning in an instant-gratifying, disposable, quick-fix, spur-of-the-moment, carpe-diem mentality! It's all about "now, now, now" and "me, me, me." It's no wonder we have difficulty coming to terms with the concept of "long-lasting." Endurance—it evokes toughing it out and waiting it out. These two things coupled together are sure to yield a positive outcome. You've surely had the treat of hearing an elderly loved one recanting the old "hard work pays off" story. It is totally true. Like all things, if something is of great value, it comes at great expense. Love is a long-term investment—and like any other, time and work are what yield a mature harvest. Nothing worthwhile comes quick or easy!

Dynamics of a Flourishing Marriage

In a previous chapter, we covered the importance of having a mission and vision statement for your marriage—this section touched on some basic concepts to consider and discuss as a couple before getting hitched. This section takes it a step further and delves into the deeper facets of individual beliefs and personalities to be examined.

Much like an onion, a relationship has many layers. Consider the heart of the onion to be your theological views. Your theology and worldview is the foundation of your relationship. God is in the center. Just as both parties following different religious systems would cause conflict in a relationship, one must also consider the next layer of the proverbial onion: your ideological views—this encompasses your political views (or lack thereof), lifestyle, parenting styles, interests, and hobbies. These factors are very close to our individuality. Although it is true that opposites can and do attract, it is necessary that at some point in our diversities, our paths converge. It is important to emphasize the difference between *opposites* and *complementary*. What we often mean when we say "opposites attract" is that we bring out the best in each other. We aren't walking in opposite directions. Our unique differences actually reinforce each other's weaknesses. On the other hand, if you are completely opposite, you will end up repelling each other. There needs to be common ground, a convergence. "Can two walk together except they agree?" (Amos 3:3).

Consider this scenario of two very different people who complement each other beautifully: Grace is introspective and quiet. She loves to listen to Steven speak. She is drawn by his wit and boldness. Steven is fun-loving, is loud, loves to socialize and get her out of her shell. They both serve together at the local soup kitchen at their church and enjoy engaging with their community. This is one of the ways they connect on a spiritual level.

In contrast, this scenario is a little more bleak—these two are so opposite they repel each other: Travis is a workaholic. He doesn't really have many interests outside work. He spends whatever little time off he has in front of the television or working on his car. He has no sense of adventure and follows a very dull, regimented lifestyle. He is very easy to please, but it's like pulling teeth for his wife to attempt engaging him in any of her interests. Linda, on the other hand, is quite boisterous and jovial and has a zest for life. She has a myriad of interests and hobbies; she loves to dance, she has a knack for the culinary arts, and she enjoys travelling. She prides herself in having a deep spiritual connection to God, while Travis shuts down any opportunity to dialogue about "religious matters." Though they claim there is love in the relationship, Linda feels trapped in her own skin. She feels as though her true self hasn't been able to come out in decades. This puts a real strain on their relationship, to say the least. They are like strangers living under the same roof.

Some hard questions to consider (peeling back the layers of the onion):

- ✓ What are your core theological beliefs and/or denomination?
- ✓ Is the Bible your plumb line for absolute truth and authority?
- ✓ What is your worldview and ideological views?
- ✓ Do you subscribe to conspiracy "theories"?
- ✓ What are your political views? (Trump or Clinton?)
- ✓ Do you want children?
- ✓ Are you prolife or prochoice?
- ✓ What is your health-care approach: traditional/pharmaceutical medicine or natural/crunchy alternatives?
- ✓ What are your parenting styles? Do you believe in corporal discipline or more gentle approaches?
- ✓ Do you believe in stay-at-home parenting verses a double-income home?

The above questions may seem trivial to some, but the complete opposite is true. They impact and shape our lives in more ways than we can imagine. If these discussions don't take place before entering a commitment, you can really be caught off guard later on in the relationship. This can really affect the dynamics of a marriage.

Let's consider this scenario for a moment: Stefanie and Tyler got married three years ago. Their marriage seemed fantastic. They both enjoyed travelling and were very career focused at the same time. Stefanie is a lawyer, and Tyler is a nurse, pursuing further education in a specific branch of medicine. To their surprise, Stefanie found herself pregnant. Tyler was ecstatic at the news, only to find out that Stefanie did not share the same joy. In fact, she resented her unborn child from the beginning. She was not ready for a baby. Tyler was prepared to make any sacrifice in order to accommodate the new arrival. His wife, on the other hand, in her resentment toward the pregnancy, began lamenting her career goals and recent promotion in her quest to become a partner at her law firm. She began to secretly consult with her doctor about the possibility of planning an abortion, until she finally made up her mind and brought it up to her husband.

Tyler was absolutely shattered and didn't even consider abortion an option. It never even crossed his mind.

One can only imagine how this story played out, and it certainly could not have ended well. As is evident in this scenario, the hard questions need to be discussed. It is naive to assume that because someone shares your religious affiliation, they also share the same core values. Sadly, today's Christianity has many faces. It is not surprising to find Christians with very diverse views on the issues of theology and morality. This applies to the other layers of the proverbial onion as well. Having said this, with much prayer and God's grace, it's not to say that having great ideological or lifestyle differences cannot work—but they will certainly pose a greater challenge to the relationship.

Dialogue does not have to be dead for the sake of keeping the peace. All too often, couples who have extremely opposing views tend to completely shut out each other when those topics creep up. In their attempt to quell conflicts, they are actually pushing each other further away. This will eventually affect the intimacy of the relationship. There are deep conversations welling up inside that are being stifled. Given an opportunity to express their ideas, couples can have opportunities to come to a better understanding and connect on a deeper intellectual, spiritual, and emotional level. Couples should not feel more comfortable engaging in these deeper conversations with people outside the relationship. This is a safeguard, given how easy it is to emotionally check out of the relationship. It is very common, when couples first meet, to have plenty of subject matter to talk about. Even the most mundane things seem fresh and exciting. It is not fair to each other to suddenly check out of the conversation simply because you don't see eye to eye or because the conversation doesn't seem interesting enough to you. Consider taking this as a challenge to spark meaningful and edifying dialogues. You might even learn something in the process. Remember to keep an open mind! Keeping an open mind keeps you humble and fosters respect.

Key to a Marriage: Respect and Humility

For a marriage to thrive at its maximum capacity, it must be fortified by these principles: humility and respect. They are like two sides of the same coin; respect is about having due regard or admiration for someone, whereas humility is about submitting oneself for the sake of the other. They ultimately yield the same result. It is impossible to say you love someone and not respect them. True respect pulls humility out of oneself.

> Let nothing be done through strife or vain-glory; but in lowliness of mind let each esteem other better than themselves. (Philippians 2:3 KJV)

Respect is the basic minimum requirement needed in order to coexist in any relationship. It starts with you, in fact! If you can't respect yourself, you will certainly not have the ability to respect your spouse—or anyone else for that matter. Think about it; when someone doesn't respect themselves, they only self-inflict harm. This comes in many forms—substance abuse, promiscuity, and self-mutilation, to name a few. Your body is a temple (1 Corinthians 6:19).

Respect is a fundamental principle that governs every facet of society. From childhood, we are taught this basic principle of respect. In the workplace, one must respect the dress code, the rules and regulations, and their schedules; otherwise, they end up unemployed. Respect must be applied to traffic laws; if you choose to disregard them, you could bring harm to yourself and those around you. There are consequences that follow. Need I bring up what happens when you disrespect law enforcement?

If all these relationships and scenarios require respect, how much more the marriage relationship? Coupled with respect, there needs to be humility. If love is the heart of the marriage, then respect and humility are the blood that pumps through it, so to speak. There is a constant inner conflict inside all of us. There is what we ought to do and what we want to do (Galatians 5:17). When we strive for what we ought to do and listen to the prompting of the Holy Spirit that lives inside us, we are able to defeat the selfish aspects of our nature that cause us to lack respect. Interestingly enough, the fruit of the spirit reflects similar attributes of what love is (1 Corinthians 13:4–7). Without love, there cannot be respect or humility.

> But the fruit of the Spirit is love, joy, peace, longsuffering, kindness, goodness, faithfulness, gentleness, self-control. Against such there is no law. (Galatians 5:22–23)

Notice the reference made pertaining to the moral law. In other words, the scripture tells us that anything contrary to the fruit of the spirit leads to chaos.

Respect goes a long way. Mutual respect is not just a one-time decision—it is a lifetime of perpetual discovery. Throughout your journey together as a couple, you are constantly learning to understand each other on every level. It challenges you to be intentional about esteeming your spouse above yourself. Respect does not undermine or overstep its boundaries. When respect is reciprocal, it creates balance in every aspect of the marriage—such as in conversation, decision-making, expressing of ideas, and your roles, to name a few. There will be times when you don't see eye to eye on everything—but when there is respect, you can both choose to agree to disagree. Respect emotionally safeguards the marriage. If respect is not kept in check, it can cause a vicious cycle of hurt, defensive reaction, and guilt. Disrespect also fuels offense. This is where the other aspect of respect comes in—humility. It is humility that softens the heart and crushes pride and bitterness. It causes you to overlook the other's faults and focus on the good. It is a peacemaker and gentle in nature. Earlier we addressed the inner conflict we face due to our fallen human nature. Humility defies human nature because it is a Christlike quality. It took humility for Christ to go to the cross and die (Philippians 2:8). Likewise, there is an aspect of death that comes with humility—death to self.

> I affirm, by the boasting in you which I have in Christ Jesus our Lord, *I die daily* [emphasis added]. (1 Corinthians 15:31)

As Paul affirms in the above scripture, we must die daily. This is a perpetual decision that requires a great deal of humility. Respecting each other in humility is no different from honoring God.

Even though you are being encouraged to die daily, there will be times where you will struggle with the thought of "How much more do I need to die to myself?" That is to be expected. The answer lies in the words *death* and *daily*. It is a perpetual process. While in the process, it is vital that you pray for the softening of your heart and for that of your spouse.

Ezekiel 36:26 tells us straight from God's Word: *"A new heart also I will give you, and a new spirit I'll put within you: and I will take away the stony heart out of your flesh, and I will give you a heart of flesh."*

This promise that God made to his people, through the prophet Jeremiah, still rings true today. You can grab a hold of this truth for your marriage. God honors his promises—they never return void. Even when you have done all the right things and aren't seeing the desired results, trust God in the process. Be persistent and intentional in prayer for the Holy Spirit to complete his work both of your hearts. It will always happen in God's timing, not yours!

You may have already heard some of these words at your own wedding ceremony, if not at someone else's:

> "Communication is important."
> "Learn to listen to each other."
> "Learn to forgive each other."
> "Share everything."
> "Laugh a lot."
> "Don't give up on each other."
> "Celebrate all that's still to come."
> "Marriage takes work, optimism, and commitment."
> "Be each other's best friend."

"Never stop loving each other."

None of those kind words ever make sense at that moment when reality kicks in. Reality is the defining moment that tests what your marriage is truly made of. Above all, respect and humility are the lifeline that nourishes the marriage. It is essential that couples build a standard of respect throughout the life of their marriage. Respect breeds environments of healthy coexistences. This standard could create a paradigm shift in marriage as we know it.

Life is a journey; relish the moments—both good and bad.

Assignment:

What are some of your core beliefs that define your identity? Does your world view conflict with that of your significant other?

_____

_____

Based on what you have read, what steps can you take in order to reconcile your differences?

_____

_____

Cassidy's Testimony

It was at twenty-two years old, fresh into my third year of college that I met my ex. We were deeply in love at the time—or so we thought. During the times we were courting, I can still remember the numerous red lights that popped up in our relationship. Suffice it to say, we ignored them all and went on doing what was right in our own eyes. We were young and ambitious with a zest for life. Some of these red lights were as follows: Both my parents and my pastor at the time told me not to pursue marriage with this young lady. My parents were in a difficult position because their son was determined to marry, regardless of whether they approved or not. As my pastor, she was privy to the family history of my fiancée. She was also concerned with the lack of sincerity my fiancée showed in her relationship with the Lord. To say the least, as my spiritual leader, she did not approve for those and other reasons she didn't divulge.

Also at the time, I had a previous ex who showed up out of nowhere. This was causing obvious frictions between my fiancée and me. As a result, we privately called off the engagement (she gave me back my popcorn ring). We still loved each other and talked a lot about spending forever together. We tried numerous attempts to resolve our issues, and we did—or so we thought. I had pursued her with all my heart (as any man would) because I wanted nothing more than to win back her trust and assured her the other woman was history and would never bother us again. My fiancée was a very resentful person, and she carried that behavior into our marriage life. I don't think she ever got over the issue with the incident with my previous ex.

My fiancée had a substance-abuse problem that never got dealt with. To make matters worse, not only did we not purse premarital counseling, I don't recall ever praying and seeking God's heart concerning our lives together. We did it our way. All these red lights among others were ignored by both of us.

Fast-forward to the spring of May 2005, the wedding took place, and we went on living our lives together. In getting married, I sincerely wanted to do the right thing. I was raised in a respectable Christian home, where my siblings and I were taught what it meant to serve the Lord with all our hearts. I didn't want to keep courting this young lady with no hope for a future. I was feeling the pressure on every side. I especially respected the roles I played in the church and wanted to be an example to those watching. We were a part of a new congregation at this point, as a way of turning over a new page in our lives. These were exciting times. She had just given her heart to Jesus, and we were on our way to bigger and better things—or so we thought.

I was a vibrant young Christian person servicing in the church as a worship pastor. I did everything I knew then to get her motivated like I was about the things of God, to no avail. Though well intended, as time went on, it would only frustrate the matter. We would have conversations from time to time about the possibility of starting a family, and even that was shunned upon by her. She was too career focused to even entertain the thought. Our life together was a mess. We were young and blinded by our egos. Everything seemed rosy from the outside but was decaying from within. We looked like a power couple but had a lot of power struggles between us. I couldn't seem to hold down a job for longer than three months at a time, and that also brought great contentions in the home. I was heavily pursuing music as I committed myself wholeheartedly toward my dreams. We just could not get it together.

By this stage, I should have gotten the fame we both dreamed of from my musical career. No such luck occurred. To make matters worse, that church gig lasted only for a couple of years, and then we moved on to another church, where I also served as the worship pastor. Again, I plunged myself into servicing the best way I knew how, and somehow, I just couldn't get her to serve faithfully alongside me. I felt at times I was doing everything to please her while failing all at the same time. In retrospect, I was trying to please her more than God himself. She became my focus, a project, if you may. All my admirations and attention was on her. I was on a quest to save our marriage. It was a real struggle, to say the least. I just couldn't reconcile, as a Christian, that a holy God would sanction divorce where we were concerned. Surely this couldn't be his will?

I was wrong! Things became more and more evident to the both of us that something was deeply wrong. In her repeated absence, people at church would often ask about her out of genuine concern. Each time, I would cover for her. I never believed in the notion of exposing one's spouse—just because. As bad as things were about to get, I understood what it meant to shield the integrity of my spouse. So I made several excuses for her. I wanted to protect our marriage and what was left of it. I was very naive in thinking that we would get through it all, but clearly I was wrong. I thought we were doing all the right things. I pleaded with her and asked that we get some help, but it became abundantly clear that I was the only one who thought that way. In fact, on many occasions, she said counseling would only benefit me and not her. She became reclusive, our romance dried up, and she would only go to church when she felt like it. She knew how much it meant to me that we go to church as a family, but she was determined to get out. She mentioned several times that she was beginning to resent me for the very thing she fell in love with me for—my passion for music and the things of God. We began growing further apart.

She started pursuing music also in a different way. She went into music engineering. I believe this was her attempt to mesh our interests, but it was too late in the game. Emotionally, she had left our marriage. At this point, she was staying over after work with friends until late into the night. I finally had enough and decided to go on a fast. I wanted answers desperately from the Lord. I needed to know his will in this matter once and for all.

One night, she got home drunk at 4:00 a.m. I had called her phone for several hours prior with no response. I noticed a car pull up by our apartment building. She was dropped off by a strange guy I had never seen before. That was the first time I witnessed another man kissing my wife, who seemed okay with the whole event. I was deeply hurt. We had a huge argument about it. She apologized, and I was open and willing to get beyond it all, until she was checking her email that morning and left her email opened. There was a trail of email between her and this person from work, which I found suspicious. They are too explicit to mention. We had a second argument about that, and things kept revealing themselves as I pressed on in fasting and prayer.

Shortly after that, she quit her job and took on a four-month contract to do some marketing promo for another company. This was her chance to finally get away. She made mention of her plans to leave for this trip when everything was already confirmed. Her mind was set. I had no chance of convincing her that this trip would not be good for what was left of our marriage. In fact, she convinced herself that this was needed.

I did all I could to save our marriage at that point. I was running low on options. I applied for a loan at the bank, and it was granted. I thought I would give it one final push. I booked a vacation, with hopes we would spend some needed time together away from it all. We did everything to recoup the depleted fuel of our relationship. And even that didn't work. It was the most expensive trip we'd ever taken. Even that couldn't buy us time or even genuine love.

When I think back on all this, it is safe to say my divorce was much cheaper than all my efforts combined trying to save my marriage. It was in that moment, when it all came crashing down, that I had a divine encounter with the Lord Jesus (another story all on its own). Throughout the moments I was fasting and praying to God for a sign and for answers, my faith in God became rock-solid. Of all the things that were exposed in those moments, the Lord was also exposing our hearts.

After our divorce was final, I began to feel this deep sense of loss. As time went on and rumors of my divorce became public knowledge, I began to feel judged by others in the church. Perhaps that was my own insecurities causing me to feel that way. I was looking for someone who understood what I was experiencing, but there was no one who could relate. Who encourages the encourager when the encourager needs encouragement? I wrestled with that question for a while within myself. I had to dig deep into my spirit at times for the comfort and assurance I was seeking. I became a statistic, and I wanted to run as far away as I possibly could. I would often encourage others of the goodness of God and the comfort of his presence. Indeed God is faithful. He confirmed that fact to me in those very tough moments. God truly never leaves us. Surely, there is a real stigma concerning divorce in the church—and I became its victim. Those who find themselves in this devastating place are often looked at as a failure. It is shunned upon, especially by the older generation. For the first time, I felt the reality of shame and brokenness. I was in a state of mourning. A part of me died. It was a devastating feeling. The feeling of loneliness started ripping at my soul. Yet I kept going after God's will for my life. I kept serving, I kept singing, I kept encouraging, but I was doing it out of a place of hurt. I was ministering out of my pain. I became worn-out over time, as I was performing in my own strength.

Finally, I thought running away would solve my deep soul issues for sure. I left the country for a while, traveling, in an attempt to dull my pain. Eventually, I joined a Christian rock band called Havenstance; we did quite a bit of travelling together both in Canada and the US. This band gave me an opportunity to get away yet to continue to serve in ministry. Throughout this time, many lives were being touched, but I was still broken inside. As a result, I fell into sin. I was weak. This brought me yet again to a very low place. This situation rehashed a lot of old memories I just wanted to delete from my mind. I could run from others, but I was having a hard time running from my internal struggles. God was still working on the inside.

Thoughts flooded my mind with memories of churches I had served and the countless lives that were impacted. I had no regrets when I thought about the eternal rewards thereof, but I certainly couldn't reconcile how I ended up where I was. I was broke and busted. I was homeless, for the most part. I went from one sibling's house to the next. I knew in my spirit that God had told me to go back home to my parents' house, but I convinced myself that couldn't be God's voice. After all, I had spent all my life building other peoples' ministry, yet I felt unaccomplished in my own skin. I started to become jaded to what I was hearing coming from the church and its leaders. My heart was consumed with pride, but I could not see it. No matter how many times it was told to me by others, I just didn't get it. However, it became clear to me that I wasn't as strong as I thought—I began having thoughts of giving up on traditional church, as it were. Everything that I thought gave me validation was stripped away from me. There was no escape. God got me exactly where he wanted me.

This was the moment when I finally came to my senses. I got stopped directly in my tracks, and all that was left to do was surrender to God. Besides, I felt full—full of all the garbage the world could offer me. I wanted nothing more than to be emptied out and be refilled by God's Holy Spirit. I repented before the Lord and placed all my selfish ambitions at his feet, and I pleaded with him to take my broken pieces and do what he pleases.

Fast-forward to 2014—I married my beautiful wife, Daniela. We have two wonderful children together, Eden and Caleb, as well as a stepson, Daniel. They have been God's sure sign that he is in the business of making all things new. He has processed me, he has tested my character, he has given me a new identity, and indeed he has restored everything the devil had stolen. He continues his work in me, and for this I am grateful. My experiences have taught me how to now be a better husband and father to the family that God has entrusted me with. I now understand that I am the head and the priest of my home. God has turned my sorrows into joy and has given me beauty for ashes. I am not proud of my divorce, but I am thankful for who it has made me today. All the glory belongs to God.

Daniela's Testimony

I'll begin my story with a little background information for better context.

I was raised in a Christian household. Sadly, my parents' marriage deteriorated after twenty-five years of "sticking it out for the kids." Things grew progressively worse until they divorced by the time I was nineteen. In the midst of the family drama, I found refuge in a romantic relationship with a young man I met at my church youth group at fifteen years old. I believed with every fiber of my being that we were going to get married. So I caved to the intense emotions I felt for him, crossed boundaries, and betrayed the values that were deeply instilled in me from a young age. By the time I had realized his chivalry was only a facade, it was too late. Before long, my first love broke my heart. I was sixteen years old, my innocence had been stolen, and I felt worthless, ashamed, dirty, and violated. In addition, I had been disillusioned by church in general; a bad breakup, friendships gone sour, betrayals, and wrong expectations pretty much summed it up. Rather than seeking God's grace, I victimized myself by these experiences, and my faith became jaded, diluted. I decided to leave the church. I clung to my Christian beliefs by a thread but had become spiritually rebellious, in a sense. I created my own version of Christianity; I played by my own rules. Fast-forwarding to eighteen years old, I still tried to be a good girl but decided to play with fire—again. Little did I know the repercussions of the choices I was about to make for years to come.

It started innocently; I was online, in chat rooms, learning to speak Spanish. My passion for the language pushed me to excellence. I was doing pretty well—well enough to meet a very nice Hispanic guy who also went to the same college I was attending. One day, I obliged to his offer to meet up for a coffee. It was then that he introduced me to meet his group of friends.

Red flag number 1: After introducing me to one guy in particular, he quietly let me know that he was "no good" because his girlfriend and mother of his six-month-old baby had recently died. He was angry with life and didn't show women much respect.

Although I had no plans to hook up with anyone, no less him, the harmless finesse in his kind gestures and bashful glances seemed to tell a different story. Over some time, this group became my friends on a casual basis. I figured I could continue being a Christian and still go out with nonbelievers. Why not? I was strong and disciplined enough. I had learned from my previous mistakes. A little compromise couldn't hurt anybody, right? I was wrong by a long shot.

This is where my first marriage story begins. Initially, I flirted with the idea of just having some innocent fun. After all, I didn't plan on either getting romantically involved or getting into a relationship with anyone. Or so I had told myself. That was until he wooed me with his Cuban charm and swept me off my feet.

You guessed it—the same guy I had been warned about. But he was so sweet! Plus, after all he had gone through and being left a single dad, I was pretty sure his friend's assessment of him was misrepresented, at best, and off by a mile. At least I was convinced. He pursued me and made me feel special. Boy was I naive. After all, my experience with the Christian type had left a bitter taste in my mouth. Perhaps giving an unbeliever a chance wasn't so bad.

It didn't take long before we had become an item. Things moved along rather quickly, even though we had originally planned on only staying friends and pretty much spent most of our outings in social gatherings. Nonetheless, the relationship progressed to a physical one, despite my resistance for some time. I gave in. During this time, we didn't dialogue too long or in depth about our worldviews. Conversations of this nature stayed rather surfaced. Perhaps it was due to the white noise of house, Latin, and reggaetton beats constantly drowning us out. After all, we hit the night scene a lot, which was very new to me. Or on second thought, maybe it was my subconscious attempt to suppress the blaring torment of my conscience. Probably the latter.

He had briefly talked to me about the death of his baby's mother, but it was very difficult for him; and in my inexperience dealing with grief, I didn't want to push the issue. Nonetheless, my compassion for him grew, and I embarked on this unfamiliar journey with him.

I let curiosity get the best of me as I explored this new and once-forbidden territory: clubs, pubs, billiard halls, casinos, alcohol, and cigarettes. It wasn't like I was a lush or anything—just a little sip here and a little drag there. But then the sips became gulps and the drags became puffs. My clothes became tighter and shorter. I couldn't be the only nerdy girl at the club, right? I eventually turned down the volume of my conscience, then gradually more, to a deafening halt. I had convinced myself that my dabbling was just an innocent bout of curiosity—an almost scientific observation of sorts.

However, it didn't take me long to realize that this guy I was with was quite heavily into drinking, hard partying, and gambling weekend after weekend. Nonetheless, I ignored my convictions and all the red flags. It soon became abundantly clear that he had a very short fuse. The intrigue of his Latin enchantment began to wear off. He cursed like a trucker and snapped at the slightest disagreement. This became obvious even in his sober state. The pain and disillusionment began to sink in, yet I still felt an obligation to stay committed. By this point, I was head over heels in love (or so I believed) and had accepted that this was what I had signed up for. I don't know whether this was due to my extreme naivety, my low self-esteem, my spiritual guilt, or the fact that he had brainwashed me into believing it—or all the above. He constantly made it a point of duty to remind me that this is who he was when I met him and this is who he is and will always be. He wasn't going to change. My fate was sealed.

As things got more serious, I attempted to engage him in conversation about deeper topics. His view of God and the world was bleak and quite cynical, so he often tried to steer clear of religious talks, despite my persistence. I was aware that he had a broken past and hadn't healed from previous life traumas, so I continued to excuse his behavior. At one point, it had become clear that breaking up was the right thing to do, but I couldn't bring myself to do it. Instead, I justified my decision by turning him into my project. I made it my mission to fix him.

As I compromised my values and priorities for the sake of salvaging the remaining shreds of this relationship, he became my drug. I had practically idolized him to the status of a demigod. As if things weren't volatile enough, I found myself pregnant at nineteen years old. Even after plugging my spiritual ears, a thread of conviction was still audible enough to remind me of the mess I was in. It was bad enough I was living in fornication—ending the relationship was not an option. Although we didn't marry right away, I had resigned to our common law lifestyle.

We eventually tied the knot, as I grasped for any crumb of hope for a better future for our family; yet breakup after breakup and empty promise after empty promise, nothing had changed. Over the years, our relationship was rocky at best. I sank deeper into despair at the realization that the man I had married was emotionally and psychologically abusive—even physically on a few occasions. We constantly struggled financially. Gambling, partying, smoking, drinking, cursing, name-calling, belittling, lavish spending—signs and clues of infidelity kept stacking up and began to take a toll on me. I was a constant emotional, paranoid, and insecure wreck, drowning in feelings of unworthiness and shame, condemnation.

I couldn't fix him or satisfy him. We fought viciously. I cried most days, all in the presence of our little boy. It broke my heart, and I despised the person I had become. I was filled with anger, sadness, distrust, bitterness, and hopelessness. My faith had become so weak that I began to question and challenge my Christian worldview, which had become skewed at best. In an attempt to escape my harsh reality, I became enchanted by the New Age philosophy and the occult, partly to mask the guilt of raising a son while clinging to a hopelessly dysfunctional relationship and as an attempt to numb the pain that was gnawing at my heart and sanity. I longed for some emotional and spiritual healing, meaning, something bigger than myself and my heap of problems. In that process, I had emotionally checked out of the relationship.

Shortly thereafter, I decided to end the relationship as it had become overwhelmingly toxic and especially unsafe for the well-being of our son. After a very drawn-out and painful divorce, I began to find some semblance of peace, living as a hardworking single mother. It gave me a renewed sense of strength and purpose to dig deeper for meaning and truth. It was in this quest that I was led back to Christ. At that point, I made the decision to *totally* surrender my life to Jesus. I was even prepared to remain single and celibate for the rest of my life, if that was my calling. It wasn't until I was ready to *totally* surrender every single area of my life to Christ that true healing would begin.

He worked in the most unimaginable ways. I noticed such a drastic transformation happening within me—from the inside out, from the way I viewed myself and others, as well as my interests. It was as if God had pressed the Reset button on my soul. I was a new person. For the first time in an eternally long phase of my life, I began to value myself. I saw myself as God saw me, and I was overwhelmed with a deep compassion for people. This longing led me to volunteer with my eleven-year-old son at an inner-city food bank run by a very small church I had begun attending. There it happened. It was at the most unpredictable timing and unexpected setting—four years after my dreadful divorce, in a small congregation with forty members or less, mainly middle-aged or elderly, in a tiny, musty, decrepit, old building. In a dingy, poorly run food bank, my divine appointment with my knight in shining armor awaited. Who would have guessed it? Alas, I was not destined for a Pauline calling. My single days were over.

God gave both of us confirmation, time and time again, that we were meant for each other. Our past experiences were so similar it was almost surreal. Our interests were strikingly in sync. But most importantly, our love for the Lord and passion to do his will was (and is) number one on both of our priority lists. This was what attracted us most to each other as we fell deeper and deeper in love. Seven months later, we wedded.

I firmly believe this is the most important component of any relationship. Putting Christ in the center has totally changed everything—and it's supposed to. He transforms us, our lives, and the lives of those we touch. I have seen undeniable evidence of this throughout our current marriage. We are certainly not perfect, but God's grace has completely taken over our lives. Although I am still learning, he has shown me what it means to be a woman, a mother, and a wife in a whole new light. He has taught me to lean on him in every aspect of our marriage. The journey is exciting, suspenseful, and adventurous. Despite life's ups and downs, we grow deeper in love, joy, and strength because we know that God has a divine purpose for our lives and for our marriage.

In retrospect, there are so many things I could have done differently, which would have avoided so much heartache, so much pain. No matter how far back I rewind, my choices could have yielded a much-better outcome had they been different and biblically guided. If I go as far back as my first relationship, a lot of the baggage from that scenario alone could have totally changed the course of my future. If I fast-forward a little to my second serious relationship, simply heeding the red flags and ending the relationship could have seriously redirected my future for the better. Even if I fast-track to the middle of my first marriage, I could have done things differently on my end, despite the dysfunctional behavior I was being dished out.

The point I want to make is that I am responsible for the consequences of my *own* actions. I don't want to dwell too long on the what-ifs and what could have been. I won't advocate for divorce because God *hates* it. Could divorce have been avoided in my situation? All I am going to say is that with God, *all* things are possible. Was I trusting in God at the time? No. I tried doing life in my own strength, despite all my best efforts. The problem lies precisely in that phrase: *my* efforts. Had I done things God's way, somewhere along the line, things would have surely turned out differently. How? I cannot say, but most definitely for the better.

Rolling forward to this day, I can only look back and see a great learning experience. In spite of all the errors I made and pitfalls I could have avoided, one thing is for sure: God is good. He is the master restorer. He works with the broken pieces you give him. He doesn't scold and berate you with condemnation over what you could have or should have done differently. He convicts, not condemns. He restores, not punishes, those who are his. Does this mean all our problems will go away? Absolutely not! We will still have to deal with the consequences of our actions, sometimes temporarily and sometimes for the rest of our lives. However, the difference is that God restores our hearts, our relationships, and our lives as he gives us the grace to move forward. He provides us with twenty-four-hour tools and support to navigate through life: prayer and his Word!

About the Author

Cassidy and Daniela started their journey together as two simple individuals. He is a Christian recording artist, songwriter, prison ministry volunteer, and blue-collar worker; while his wife, Daniela, is a stay-at-home mother of three and avid blogger. They have coauthored this book as a result of their experiences and their passion for seeing other couples discover God's greatest potential for their marriages.

.

CPSIA information can be obtained
at www.ICGtesting.com
Printed in the USA
LVHW04s0912120818
586653LV00002B/3/P